THE

WRITINGS

OF

S. S. PETER, JAMES, AND JOHN;

TOGETHER WITH

NOTICES OF THEIR LIVES,

AND

THE TEN COMMANDMENTS.

THE TEXT ACCURATELY COPIED FROM AN EDITION OF THE DOWAY BIBLE, REVISED AND CORRECTED ACCORDING TO THE CLEMENTINE EDITION OF THE SCRIPTURES, WITH THE APPROBATION OF THE

MOST REV. JOHN HUGHES,

ARCHBISHOP OF NEW YORK.

LITHOTYPED BY THE AMERICAN STEREOTYPE COMPANY,
PHŒNIX BUILDING, BOSTON.

DEO REIPUBLICÆ ET AMICIS
George Duffield A.M
In tali nunquam lassat venatio sylva.
A.D.1884.

THE HOLY BIBLE,

TRANSLATED FROM THE LATIN VULGATE.

The Old Testament was first published by the English College at Doway, A. D. 1609, and the New Testament by the English College at Rheims, A. D., 1582.)

REVISED AND CORRECTED, ACCORDING TO THE

CLEMENTINE EDITION OF THE SCRIPTURES,

WITH THE APPROBATION OF

THE MOST REV. JOHN HUGHES,

ARCHBISHOP OF NEW YORK.

THE BOOK OF EXODUS.

CHAP. XX. v. 1–2. And the Lord spoke all these words: I am
the Lord thy God, who brought thee out of
3 the land of E-gypt, out of the house of bond-age. Thou
4 shalt not have strange gods be-fore me. Thou shalt
not make to thy-self a grav-en thing, nor the like-ness
of any thing that is in heav-en a-bove, or in the earth
be-neath, nor of those things that are in the wa-ters
5 un-der the earth. Thou shalt not a-dore them, nor
serve *them:* I am the Lord thy God, migh-ty, jeal-ous,
vis-it-ing the in-iqui-ty of the fa-thers up-on the children, un-to the third and fourth gen-e-ra-tion of them
6 that hate me: And show-ing mer-cy un-to thous-ands
to them that love me, and keep my com-mand-ments.
7 Thou shalt not take the name of the Lord thy God
in vain: for the Lord will not hold him guilt-less that
shall take the name of the Lord his God in vain.
8 Re-mem-ber that thou keep ho-ly the sab-bath day.
9 Six days shalt thou la-bour, and shalt do all thy works.
10 But on the sev-enth day is the sab-bath of the Lord
thy God: thou shalt do no work on it, thou, nor thy
son, nor thy daugh-ter, nor thy man-ser-vant, nor thy
maid-ser-vant, nor thy beast, nor the stran-ger that is

11 with-in thy gates. For in six days the Lord made
heav-en and earth and the sea, and all things that
are in them, and rest-ed on the sev-enth day: therefore the Lord bless-ed the sev-enth day, and sanc-ti-fied
12 it. Hon-our thy fa-ther and thy moth-er, that thou
may-est be long liv-ed upon the land which the
13 Lord thy God will give thee. Thou shalt not kill.
14–15 Thou shalt not com-mit a-dul-te-ry. Thou shalt not
16 steal. Thou shalt not bear false wit-ness a-gainst thy
17 neigh-bour. Thou shalt not cov-et thy neigh-bour's
house: nei-ther shalt thou de-sire his wife, nor his
ser-vant, nor his hand-maid, nor his ox, nor his ass, nor
18 any thing that is his. And all the peo-ple saw the
voi-ces, and the flames, and the sound of the trump-et,
and the mount smok-ing: and be-ing ter-ri-fied and
19 struck with fear, they stood a-far off, Say-ing to
Mo-ses: Speak thou to us, and we will hear: let not
20 the Lord speak to us, lest we die. And Mo-ses said
to the peo-ple: Fear not; for God is come to prove
you, and that the dread of him might be in you, and
you should not sin.

THE HOLY GOSPEL OF JESUS CHRIST ACCORDING TO ST. JOHN.

CHAP. I. v. 1–2. In the be-gin-ning was the Word, and the Word
was with God, and the Word was God. The
3 same was in the be-gin-ning with God. All things were
made by him: and without him was made noth-ing that
4 was made. In him was life; and the life was the
5 light of men. And the light shin-eth in dark-ness; and
6 the dark-ness did not com-pre-hend it. There was a
7 man sent from God, whose name was John. This
man came for a wit-ness, to bear wit-ness of the light,
8 that all men might be-lieve through him. He was not
9 the light, but was to bear wit-ness of the light. That
was the true light, which en-light-en-eth every man that
10 com-eth in-to this world. He was in the world, and
the world was made by him; and the world knew him
11 not. He came un-to his own; and his own re-ceiv-ed
12 him not. But as ma-ny as re-ceiv-ed him, to them he
gave pow-er to be made the sons of God, to them that
13 be-lieve in his name: Who are born, not of blood,

nor of the will of the flesh, nor of the will of man, but
14 of God. And the word was made flesh, and dwelt
among us: and we saw his glory the glory as of the
only begotten of the Father, full of grace and truth.
15 John beareth witness of him: and crieth out, saying:
This was he of whom I spake: He that shall come
after me, is preferred before me, because he was be-
16 fore me. And of his fulness we all have received,
17 and grace for grace. (For the law was given by
18 Moses: grace and truth came by Jesus Christ.) No
man hath seen God at any time: the only begotten
Son, who is in the bosom of the Father, he hath de-
19 clared him. And this is the testimony of John,
when the Jews sent from Jerusalem priests and Levites
20 to him, to ask him: Who art thou? And he confessed and did not deny: and he confessed: I am
21 not the Christ. And they asked him: What then?
Art thou Elias? And he said: I am not. Art thou the
22 prophet? And he answered: No. Then they said to
him: Who art thou, that we may give an answer to
23 them that sent us? What sayest thou of thyself? He
said: I am the voice of one crying in the wilderness:
Make straight the way of the Lord, as the Prophet
24–25 Isaias said. And they that were sent were of the Pharisees. And they that asked him, and said to him: Why
then dost thou baptize, if thou be not Christ, nor Elias,
26 nor the prophet? John answered them, saying: I baptize in water: but there hath stood one in the midst of
27 you, whom you know not. The same is he that shall
come after me, who is preferrèd before me; the latchet
28 of whose shoe I am not worthy to loose. These things
were done in Bethanias beyond the Jordan, where John
29 was baptizing. The next day John saw Jesus coming
to him; and he saith: Behold the Lamb of God; be-
30 hold, he who taketh away the sin of the world. This
is he of whom I said: After me cometh a man, who is
31 preferred before me, because he was before me. And
I knew him not: but that he may be made manifest in
32 Israel, therefore am I come baptizing in water. And
John gave testimony, saying: I saw the Spirit coming
down as a dove from heaven, and he remained upon
33 him. And I knew him not; but he, who sent me to
baptize in water, said to me: He upon whom thou

shalt see the Spirit descending, and remaining on him,
34 he it is that baptizeth with the Holy Ghost. And I
saw; and I gave testimony, that this is the Son of God.
35 Again the following day, John stood and two of his
36 disciples. And looking upon Jesus as he was walking,
37 he saith: Behold the Lamb of God. And the two
disciples heard him speak; and they followed Jesus.
38 And Jesus turning, and seeing them following him,
saith to them: What seek you? They said to him:
Rabbi, (which is to say, being interpreted, Master)
39 where dwellest thou? He saith to them: come and
see. They came, and saw where he abode; and they
staid with him that day: now it was about the tenth
40 hour. And Andrew the brother of Simon Peter was
one of the two who had heard of John, and followed
41 him. He first findeth his brother Simon, and said to
him: we have found the Messias, which is, being inter-
42 preted, the Christ. And he brought him to Jesus.
And Jesus looking upon him, said: Thou art Simon
the son of Jona: thou shalt be called Cephas: which is
43 interpreted Peter. On the following day he would go
forth into Galilee; and he findeth Philip. And Jesus
44 said to him: follow me. Now Philip was of Bethsaida,
45 the city of Andrew and Peter. Philip findeth Nathaniel, and said to him: We have found him of whom
Moses in the law, and the prophets did write, Jesus the
46 son of Joseph of Nazareth. And Nathaniel said to
him: Can any thing of good come from Nazareth?
47 Philip saith to him: Come and see. Jesus saw Nathaniel coming to him; and he saith of him: Behold
48 an Israelite indeed, in whom there is no guile. Nathaniel said to him: Whence knowest thou me? Jesus
answered and said to him: Before that Philip called
thee, when thou wast under the fig-tree, I saw thee.
49 Nathaniel answered him and said: Rabbi, thou art the
50 Son of God; thou art the King of Israel. Jesus
answered, and said to him: Because I said unto thee,
I saw thee under the fig-tree, thou believest: greater
51 things than these shalt thou see. And he saith to him:
Amen, amen I say to you, you shall see the heaven
opened, and the angels of God ascending and descending upon the Son of man.

CHAP. II. } And the third day there was a marriage in Cana
v. 1. } of Galilee; and the mother of Jesus was there.
2 And Jesus also was invited, and his disiples, to the
3 marriage. And the wine failing, the mother of Jesus
4 saith to him: They have no wine. And Jesus saith
to her: Woman, what is *that* to me and to thee?
5 my hour is not yet come. His mother saith to the
6 waiters: Whatsoever he shall say to you, do ye. Now
there were set there six water-pots of stone, according
to the manner of the purifying of the Jews, containing
7 two or three measures apiece. Jesus saith to them:
Fill the water-pots with water. And they filled them
8 up to the brim. And Jesus saith to them: Draw out
now and carry to the chief steward of the feast. And
9 they carried it. And when the chief steward had
tasted the water made wine, and knew not whence it
was, but the waiters knew who had drawn the water;
10 the chief steward called the bridegroom, And saith
to him: Every man at first setteth forth good wine;
and when men have well drank, then that which is
worse: but thou hast kept the good wine until now.
11 This beginning of miracles did Jesus in Cana of Galilee: and he manifested his glory; and his disciples
12 believed in him. After this he went down to Capharnaum, he and his mother, and his brethren, and his disci-
13 ples: and they remained there not many days. And
the pasch of the Jews was at hand: and Jesus went
14 up to Jerusalem. And he found in the temple those
that sold oxen and sheep and doves, and the changers
15 of money sitting. And when he had made as it were
a scourge of little cords, he drove them all out of the
temple, the sheep also and the oxen: and he poured
out the changers' money; and the tables he overthrew.
16 And he said to them that sold doves: Take these things
hence; and make not the house of my Father a house
17 of traffic. And his disciples remembered that it was
written: The zeal of thy house has eaten me up.
18 Then the Jews answered, and said to him: What sign
dost thou show us, seeing thou doest these things?
19 Jesus answered, and said to them: Destroy this tem-
20 ple, and in three days I will raise it up. The Jews then
said: Six and forty years was this temple in building,

21 and wilt thou raise it up in three days? But he spoke
22 of the temple of his body. When therefore he was
risen again from the dead, his disciples remembered
that he had said this: and they believed the scripture,
23 and the word that Jesus had said. Now when he was
at Jerusalem, at the pasch upon the festival day, many
believed in his name, seeing his miracles which he did.
24 But Jesus did not trust himself to them, because he
25 knew all men, And because he needed not that any
should give testimony of man: for he knew what was
in man.

CHAP. III. } And there was a man of the Pharisees, named
v. 1–2. } Nicodemus, a ruler of the Jews. This man
came to Jesus by night, and said to him: Rabbi, we
know that thou art come a teacher from God: for no
man can do these miracles which thou doest, unless
3 God was with him. Jesus answered, and said to him:
Amen, amen I say to thee, except a man be born again,
4 he cannot see the kingdom of God. Nicodemus saith
to him: How can a man be born when he is old? can
he enter the second time into his mother's womb, and
5 be born again? Jesus answered: Amen, amen I say
to thee, unless a man be born again of water and the
Holy Ghost, he cannot enter into the kingdom of God.
6 That which is born of the flesh, is flesh: and that
7 which is born of the spirit, is spirit. Wonder not that
8 I said to thee, you must be born again. The spirit
breatheth where he will; and thou hearest his voice;
but thou knowest not whence he cometh, nor whither
he goeth: so is every one that is born of the spirit.
9 Nicodemus answered, and said to him: how can these
10 things be done? Jesus answered and said to him:
Art thou a master of Israel, and knowest not these
11 things? Amen, amen I say to thee: we speak what
we know, and we testify what we have seen; and you
12 receive not our testimony. If I have spoken to you
earthly things, and you believe not, how will you be-
13 lieve if I shall speak to you heavenly things? And
no man hath ascended into heaven, but he that descen-
ded from heaven, the Son of man, who is in heaven.
14 And as Moses lifted up the serpent in the desert, so

15 must the Son of man be lifted up: That whosoever
believeth in him may not perish, but may have life
16 everlasting. For God so loved the world, as to give
his only begotten Son; that whosoever believeth in
him may not perish, but may have life everlasting.
17 For God sent not his Son into the world to judge the
18 world, but that the world may be saved by him. He
that believeth in him is not judged: but he that doth
not believe is already judged: because he believeth
not in the name of the only begotten Son of God.
19 And this is the judgment: because the light is come
into the world, and men loved darkness rather than
20 the light: for their works were evil. For every one
that doeth evil, hateth the light, and cometh not to the
21 light, that his works may not be reproved. But he
that doeth truth, cometh to the light, that his works
may be made manifest, because they are done in God.
22 After these things Jesus and his disciples came into the
land of Judea: and there he abode with them and
23 baptized. And John also was baptizing in Ennon near
Salim, because there was much water there: and they
24 came, and were baptized. For John was not yet cast
25 into prison. And there rose a question between some
of John's disciples and the Jews, concerning purifica-
26 tion. And they came to John, and said to him: Rabbi,
he that was with thee beyond the Jordan, to whom thou
gavest testimony, behold, he baptizeth, and all men
27 come to him. John answered and said: A man cannot receive any thing except it be given him from
28 heaven. You yourselves do bear me witness, that I
said, I am not the Christ, but that I am sent before
29 him. He that hath the bride, is the bridegroom: but
the friend of the bridegroom, who standeth and heareth him, rejoiceth with joy because of the bridegroom's voice. This my joy, therefore, is fulfilled.
30–31 He must increase; but I must decrease. He that
cometh from above, is above all. He that is of the
earth, of the earth he is, and of the earth he speaketh.
32 He that cometh from heaven, is above all. And what
he hath seen, and heard, that he testifieth: and no man
33 receiveth his testimony. He that hath received his
testimony, hath attested by his seal that God is true.

34 For he whom God hath sent, speaketh the words of
God: for God doth not give the Spirit by measure.
35 The Father loveth the Son: and he hath given all
36 things into his hand. He that believeth in the Son,
hath life everlasting; but he that believeth not the
Son, shall not see life; but the wrath of God abideth
on him.

CHAP. IV. } When, therefore, Jesus understood that the
v. 1. } Pharisees had heard that Jesus maketh more
2 disciples, and baptized *more* than John, (Though Jesus
3 *himself* did not baptize, but his disciples.) He left
4 Judea, and departed into Galilee. And it was necessary
5 he should pass through Samaria. He cometh, therefore, to a city of Samaria which is called Sichar; near
the piece of ground, which Jacob gave to his son
6 Joseph. Now Jacob's well was there. Jesus, therefore, being wearied with his journey, sat thus on the
7 well. It was about the sixth hour. There cometh a
woman of Samaria to draw water. Jesus saith to her:
8 Give me to drink: (For his disciples were gone into
9 the city to buy food.) Then that Samaritan woman
saith to him: How dost thou, being a Jew, ask of me
to drink, who am a Samaritan woman? For the Jews
10 do not communicate with the Samaritans. Jesus answered, and said to her: If thou didst know the gift
of God, and who it is that saith to thee, give me to
drink; thou, perhaps, wouldst have asked of him, and
11 he would have given thee living water. The woman
saith to him: Sir, thou hast nothing wherein to draw,
and the well is deep: from whence then hast thou liv-
12 ing water? Art thou greater than our father Jacob,
who gave us the well, and drank thereof himself, and
13 his children, and his cattle? Jesus answered, and said
to her: Whosoever drinketh of this water, shall thirst
again: but he that shall drink of the water that I
14 shall give him, shall not thirst forever, But the water
that I shall give him, shall become in him a fountain
15 of water, springing up unto everlasting life. The
woman saith to him: Sir, give me this water, that I
16 may not thirst, nor come hither to draw. Jesus saith
to her: Go, call thy husband and come hither.

17 The woman answered, and said: I have no husband. Jesus said to her: Thou hast said well, I
18 have no husband: For thou hast had five husbands:
and he whom thou now hast, is not thy husband. This
19 thou hast said truly. The woman saith to him: Sir,
20 I perceive that thou art a prophet. Our fathers adored
on this mountain: and you say, that at Jerusalem is
21 the place where men must adore. Jesus saith to her:
Woman, believe me, the hour cometh, when you shall
neither on this mountain nor in Jerusalem adore the
22 Father. You adore that which you know not: we
adore that which we know: for salvation is of the
23 Jews. But the hour cometh, and now is, when the
true adorer shall adore the Father in spirit and in
truth. For the Father also seeketh such to adore him.
24 God is a spirit: and they that adore him, must adore
25 him in spirit and in truth. The woman saith to him:
I know that the Messias cometh (who is called Christ:)
therefore, when he is come, he will tell us all things.
26 Jesus saith to her: I am he, who am speaking with
27 thee. And immediately his disciples came: and they
wondered that he talked with the woman. Yet no
man said: What seekest thou, or why talkest thou
28 with her? The woman, therefore, left her water-pot,
and went her way into the city, and saith to those men:
29 Come, and see a man who hath told me all things
30 that ever I did. Is not he the Christ? Then they
31 went out of the city, and came to him. In the mean
time the disciples prayed him, saying: Rabbi, eat.
32 But he said to them: I have food to eat, which you
33 know not of. The disciples, therefore, said one to
another: Hath any man brought him any thing to
34 eat? Jesus said to them: My food is to do the will
of him that sent me, that I may perfect his work.
35 Do not you say, there are yet four months, and then
the harvest cometh? Behold, I say to you, lift up
your eyes, and see the countries, for they are white
36 already to harvest. And he that reapeth, receiveth
wages, and gathereth fruit unto everlasting life; that
both he that soweth, and he that reapeth, may rejoice
37 together. For in this is the saying true; that it is
one man that soweth, and it is another that reapeth.

38 I have sent you to reap that in which you did not
labour: others have laboured and you have entered
39 into their labours. Now of that city many of the
Samaritans believed in him, for the word of the woman giving testimony, that he told me whatsoever I
40 have done. So when the Samaritans were come to
him, they desired him that he would stay there. And
41 he staid there two days. And many more believed in
42 him because of his own word. And they said to the
woman: We now believe, not for thy saying: for
we ourselves have heard him, and know that this is
43 indeed the Saviour of the world. Now after two days
44 he departed thence, and went into Galilee. For Jesus
himself gave testimony that a prophet hath not honour
45 in his own country. Then when he was come into
Galilee, the Galileans received him, having seen all
the things he had done at Jerusalem on the festival
46 day: for they also went to the festival day. He came
again therefore into Cana of Galilee, where he made
the water wine. And there was a certain ruler, whose
47 son was sick at Capharnaum. He having heard that
Jesus was come from Judea into Galilee, went to him,
and prayed him to come down and heal his son: for
48 he was at the point of death. Then Jesus said to him:
Unless you see signs and wonders, you believe not.
49 The ruler saith to him: Sir, come down before that
50 my son die. Jesus saith to him: Go thy way, thy
son liveth. The man believed the word which Jesus
51 said to him, and went his way. And as he was going
down, his servants met him: and they brought word,
52 saying that his son lived. He asked, therefore, of
them the hour, wherein he grew better. And they
said to him: Yesterday, at the seventh hour, the
53 fever left him. The father, therefore, knew that it
was at the same hour that Jesus said to him: Thy
son liveth: and himself believed, and his whole house.
54 This *is* again the second miracle that Jesus did, when
he was come out of Judea into Galilee.

CHAP. V. v. 1. After these things, there was a festival day of
the Jews, and Jesus went up to Jerusalem.
2 Now there is at Jerusalem, a pond, *called* Probatica,

which in Hebrew is named Bethsaida, having five por-
3 ches. In these lay a great multitude of sick, of blind,
of lame, of withered, waiting for the moving of the
4 water. And an angel of the Lord went down at a
certain time into the pond: and the water was moved.
And he that went down first into the pond, after the
motion of the water, was made whole of whatsoever
5 infirmity he lay under. And there was a certain man
there, that had been eight and thirty years under his
6 infirmity. Him when Jesus had seen lying, and knew
that he had been now a long time, he saith to him:
7 Wilt thou be made whole? The infirm man answered
him: Sir, I have no man, when the water is troubled,
to put me into the pond: for whilst I am coming,
8 another goeth down before me. Jesus saith to him:
9 Arise, take up thy bed, and walk. And immediately
the man was made whole: and he took up his bed, and
10 walked. And it was the sabbath that day. The
Jews, therefore, said to him that was cured: It is
the sabbath: it is not lawful for thee to take up thy
11 bed. He answered them: He that made me whole,
12 he said to me: Take up thy bed, and walk. They
asked him therefore: Who is that man that said to
13 thee: Take up thy bed, and walk? But he that
was healed knew not who it was. For Jesus went
aside from the multitude that was standing in the place.
14 Afterwards Jesus findeth him in the temple, and saith
to him: Behold, thou art made whole: sin no more,
15 lest some worse thing happen to thee. The man went
his way, and told the Jews, that it was Jesus that had
16 made him whole. Thereupon the Jews persecuted
Jesus, because he did these things on the sabbath.
17 But Jesus answered them: My Father worketh until
18 now; and I work. Hereupon, therefore, the Jews
sought the more to kill him, because he did not only
break the sabbath, but also said that God was his Father, making himself equal to God. Then Jesus an-
19 swered, and said to them: Amen, amen I say unto you:
the Son cannot do any thing of himself, but what he
seeth the Father do: for what things soever he doeth,
20 these the Son also doeth in like manner. For the
Father loveth the Son, and showeth him all things

which himself doeth; and greater works than these
21 will he show him that you may wonder. For as the
Father raiseth up the dead, and giveth life: so the Son
22 also giveth life to whom he will. For neither doth the
Father judge any man; but hath committed all judg-
23 ment to the Son: That all men may honour the Son,
as they honour the Father. He who honoureth not
the Son, honoureth not the Father who hath sent him.
24 Amen, amen I say unto you, he that heareth my word,
and believeth him that sent me, hath everlasting life;
and cometh not into judgment, but is passed from death
25 to life. Amen, amen I say unto you, that the hour
cometh, and now is, when the dead shall hear the voice
of the Son of God; and they that hear shall live.
26 For as the Father hath life in himself, so he hath
27 given to the Son also to have life in himself: And he
hath given him authority to execute judgment, because
28 he is the Son of man. Wonder not at this; for the
hour cometh, wherein all that are in the graves shall
29 hear the voice of the Son of God. And they that
have done good, shall come forth unto the resurrection
of life; but they that have done evil, unto the resur-
30 rection of judgment. I can do nothing of myself. As
I hear, so I judge: and my judgment is just: because
I seek not my own will, but the will of him that sent
31 me. If I bear witness of myself, my witness is not
32 true. There is another that beareth witness of me:
and I know that the witness which he witnesseth of
33 me is true. You sent to John: and he gave testimony
34 to the truth. But I receive not testimony from man:
35 but I say these things that you may be saved. He
was a burning and a shining lamp. And you were
36 willing for a time to rejoice in his light. But I have
a greater testimony than that of John. For the works
which the Father hath given me to perfect; the works
themselves, which I do, give testimony of me, that the
37 Father hath sent me. And the Father himself who
hath sent me, hath given testimony of me: neither
have you heard his voice at any time, nor seen his
38 shape. And you have not his word abiding in you:
39 for whom he hath sent, him you believe not. Search
the scriptures: for you think in them to have life ever-

lasting: and the same are they that give testimony of
40 me: And you will not come to me, that you may
41–42 have life. I receive not glory from men. But I know
43 you, that you have not the love of God in you. I
am come in the name of my Father: and you receive
me not. If another shall come in his own name, him
44 you will receive. How can you believe, who receive
glory one from another; and the glory which is from
45 God alone, you do not seek? Think not that I will
accuse you to the Father. There is one that accuseth
46 you, Moses, in whom you trust. For if you did
believe Moses, you would, perhaps, believe me also:
47 for he wrote of me. But if you do not believe his
writings, how will you believe my words?

CHAP. VI. } After this Jesus went over the sea of Galilee,
v. 1–2 } which is that of Tiberias: And a great multitude followed him; because they saw the miracles
3 which he did on them that were infirm. And Jesus
went up into a mountain; and there he sat with his
4 disciples. Now the pasch, the festival day of the
5 Jews, was near at hand. When Jesus, therefore, had
lifted up his eyes, and seen that a very great multitude
cometh to him, he said to Philip: Whence shall we
6 buy bread, that these may eat? And this he said to
try him; for he himself knew what he would do.
7 Philip answered him: Two hundred pennyworth of
bread is not sufficient for them, that every one may
8 take a little. One of his disciples, Andrew, the brother
9 of Simon Peter, saith to him; There is a boy here
that hath five barley loaves and two fishes; but what
10 are these among so many? Then Jesus said: Make
the men sit down. Now there was much grass in the
place. So the men sat down, in number about five
11 thousand. And Jesus took the loaves: and when he
had given thanks, he distributed to them that were set
down; in like manner also of the fishes, as much as
12 they would. And when they were filled he said to
his disciples: Gather up the fragments that remain,
13 lest they be lost. So they gathered them up, and
filled twelve baskets with the fragments of the five
barley loaves, which remained over and above to them

14 that had eaten. Then those men, when they had seen
what a miracle Jesus had done, said: This is the
15 prophet indeed, that is to come into the world. When
Jesus, therefore, perceived that they would come and
take him by force, and make him king, he fled again
16 into the mountain himself alone. And when evening
17 was come, his disciples went down to the sea. And
when they had entered into a ship, they went over the
sea to Capharnaum: and it was now dark; and Jesus
18 was not come to them. And the sea arose, by reason
19 of a great wind that blew. So when they had rowed
about five and twenty or thirty furlongs, they see Jesus
walking on the sea, and drawing near to the ship: and
20 they were afraid. But he said to them: It is I: be
21 not afraid. They were willing, therefore, to take him
into the ship: and presently the ship was at the land,
22 to which they were going. The next day, the multitude that stood on the other side of the sea, saw that
there was no other ship there but one, and that Jesus
had not entered into the ship with his disciples, but
23 that his disciples only had gone away. But other ships
came in from Tiberias, near to the place where they
24 had eaten the bread, the Lord giving thanks. When
the people, therefore, saw that Jesus was not there,
nor his disciples, they took shipping, and came to Ca-
25 pharnaum, seeking for Jesus. And when they had
found him on the other side of the sea, they said to
26 him: Rabbi, when camest thou hither? Jesus answered them and said: Amen, amen I say to you:
You seek me, not because you have seen miracles, but
because you did eat of the loaves, and were filled.
27 Labour not for the meat which perisheth, but for that
which endureth unto everlasting life, which the Son of
man will give you. For him hath God the Father
28 sealed? They said, therefore, to him: What shall we
29 do, that we may work the works of God? Jesus answered, and said to them: This is the work of God, that
30 you believe in him whom he hath sent. They said
therefore to him: What sign then dost thou show that
we may see, and may believe thee? what dost thou
31 work? Our fathers did eat manna in the desert; as it
is written: He gave them bread from heaven to eat.

32 Then Jesus said to them: Amen, amen, I say to you:
Moses gave you not bread from heaven; but my
33 Father giveth you the true bread from heaven. For
the bread of God is that which cometh down from
34 heaven, and giveth life to the world. Then they said
35 to him: Lord, give us always this bread. And Jesus
said to them: I am the bread of life: he that cometh
to me, shall not hunger: and he that believeth in me,
36 shall never thirst. But I said to you, that you also
37 have seen me, and you believed not. All that the
Father giveth me, shall come to me; and him that
38 cometh to me, I will not cast out: Because I came
down from heaven, not to do my own will, but the will
39 of him that sent me. Now this is the will of him that
sent me, the Father: that all that he hath given me, I
lose not thereof, but raise it up again at the last day.
40 And this is the will of my Father who sent me: that
every one who seeth the Son, and believeth in him,
may have everlasting life; and I will raise him up at
41 the last day. The Jews then murmured at him,
because he had said: I am the living bread which
42 came down from heaven. And they said: Is not this
Jesus the son of Joseph, whose father and mother we
know? How then saith he, I came down from
43 heaven? Jesus therefore answered, and said to them:
44 Murmur not among yourselves. No man can
come to me, except the Father, who hath sent me,
draw him: and I will raise him up at the last day.
45 It is written in the prophets: And they shall all be
taught of God. Every one that hath heard of the
46 Father, and hath learned, cometh to me. Not that any
man hath seen the Father, but he who is of God, he
47 hath seen the Father. Amen, amen I say unto you:
48 He that believeth in me, hath everlasting life. I am
49 the bread of life. Your fathers did eat manna in the
50 desert, and they died. This is the bread descending
down from heaven; that if any one eat of it, he may
51 not die. I am the living bread, which came down
52 from heaven. If any man eat of this bread, he shall
live for ever; and the bread which I will give, is my
53 flesh for the life of the world. The Jews, therefore,
debated among themselves, saying: How can this man

54 give us his flesh to eat? Then Jesus said to them,
Amen, amen I say unto you: Unless you eat the flesh
of the Son of man, and drink his blood, you shall not
55 have life in you. He that eateth my flesh, and drinketh
my blood, hath everlasting life; and I will raise him
56 up at the last day. For my flesh is meat indeed; and
57 my blood is drink indeed. He that eateth my flesh,
and drinketh my blood, abideth in me, and I in him.
58 As the living father hath sent me, and I live by the
Father; so he that eateth me, the same also shall live
59 by me. This is the bread that came down from heaven. Not as your fathers did eat manna, and died.
60 He that eateth this bread, shall live for ever. These
things he said teaching in the synagogue, in Caphar-
61 naum. Many, therefore, of his disciples hearing *it*,
62 said: This saying is hard, and who can hear it? But
Jesus, knowing in himself that his disciples murmured
63 at this, said to them: Doth this scandalize you? If
then you shall see the Son of man ascend up where
64 he was before? It is the Spirit that quickeneth:
the flesh profiteth nothing: the words that I have
65 spoken to you, are spirit and life. But there are some
of you that believe not. For Jesus knew from the
beginning who they were that did not believe, and
66 who he was that would betray him. And he said:
Therefore did I say to you, that no man can come to
67 me, unless it be given him by my Father. After this
many of his disciples went back, and walked no more
68 with him. Then Jesus said to the twelve: Will you
69 also go away? And Simon Peter answered him:
Lord, to whom shall we go? thou hast the words of
70 eternal life. And we have believed, and have known
71 that thou art the Christ the Son of God. Jesus answered them: Have not I chosen you twelve; and of
72 you one is a devil? Now he meant Judas Iscariot,
the son of Simon: for this same was about to betray
him; whereas he was one of the twelve.

CHAP. VII. v. 1. After these things Jesus walked into Galilee;
for he would not walk in Judea; because the
2 Jews sought to kill him. Now the feast of the Jews,
3 called of the tabernacles, was at hand. And his

brethren said to him: Pass from hence, and go into
Judea, that thy disciples also may see thy works which
4 thou doest. For there is no man that doeth any thing
in secret, and he himself seeketh to be known openly:
if thou do these things, manifest thyself to the world.
5–6 For neither did his brethren believe in him. Then
Jesus said to them: My time is not yet come: but
7 your time is always ready. The world cannot hate
you: but me it hateth; because I give testimony of it,
8 that the works thereof are evil. Go you up to this
festival day: but I go not up to this festival day; be-
9 cause my time is not yet fulfilled. When he had said
10 these things, he himself staid in Galilee. But after
his brethren were gone up, then he also went up to
the feast, not publickly, but as it were in private.
11 The Jews therefore sought him on the festival day,
12 and said: Where is he? And there was much murmuring among the multitude concerning him. For
some said: He is a good man. And others said: No;
13 but he seduceth the people. Yet no man spoke openly
14 of him for fear of the Jews. Now, about the midst of
the feast, Jesus went up into the temple, and taught.
15 And the Jews wondered, saying: How doth this man
16 know letters, having never learned? Jesus answered
them, and said: My doctrine is not mine, but of him
17 that sent me. If any man will do the will of him, he
shall know of the doctrine, whether it be from God,
18 or whether I speak from myself. He that speaketh
from himself, seeketh his own glory: but he that seeketh the glory of him that sent him, he is true, and there
19 is no injustice in him: Did not Moses give you the
20 law: and none of you keepeth the law? Why seek
you to kill me? The multitude answered, and said:
21 Thou hast a devil: who seeketh to kill thee? Jesus
answered, and said to them, One work I have done:
22 and you all wonder: Therefore Moses gave you circumcision: (not because it is of Moses; but of the
fathers) and on the sabbath-day you circumcise a man.
23 If a man receive circumcision on the sabbath-day, that
the law of Moses may not be broken; are you angry
at me because I have healed the whole man on the
24 sabbath-day? Judge not according to the appearance,

25 but judge a just judgment. Then some of Jerusalem
26 said: Is not this he whom they seek to kill? And,
behold, he speaketh openly; and they say nothing to
him. Have the rulers known, indeed, that this is the
27 Christ? But we know this man whence he is: but
when the Christ cometh, no man knoweth whence he
28 is. Jesus, therefore, cried out in the temple, teaching
and saying: You both know me, and you know whence
I am: and I am not come of myself: but he that sent
29 me is true, whom you know not. I know him: be-
30 cause I am from him, and he hath sent me. They
sought, therefore, to apprehend him, but no man laid
hands on him; because his hour was not yet come.
31 But of the people many believed in him, and said:
When the Christ cometh, shall he do more miracles
32 than these which this man doeth? The Pharisees
heard the people murmuring these things concerning
him: and the rulers and Pharisees sent ministers to
33 apprehend him. Jesus, therefore, said to them: Yet
a little while I am with you: and I go to him that sent
34 me. You shall seek me, and shall not find me: and
35 where I am, you cannot come. The Jews, therefore,
said among themselves: Whither will he go, that we
shall not find him? will he go to the dispersed among
36 the Gentiles, and teach the Gentiles? What is this
saying that he hath said: You shall seek me, and shall
37 not find me: and where I am you cannot come? Now
on the last great day of the festivity, Jesus stood and
cried out, saying: If any man thirst, let him come to
38 me, and drink. He that believeth in me, as the Scripture saith, Out of his belly shall flow rivers of living
39 water. Now this he said of the spirit which they
should receive who believed in him: for as yet the
spirit was not given; because Jesus was not yet glori-
40 fied. Of that multitude, therefore, when they had
heard these words of his, some said: This is the
41 prophet indeed. Others said: This is the Christ. But
some said: Doth the Christ come out of Galilee?
42 Doth not the Scripture say: That Christ cometh of
the seed of David, and out of Bethlehem, the town
43 where David was? So there arose a dissension among
44 the people because of him. And some of them would

have apprehended him: but no man laid hands upon
45 him. So the ministers came to the chief priests and
the Pharisees. And they said to them: Why have
46 you not brought him? The ministers answered:
47 Never did man speak like this man. Then the Phari-
48 sees answered them: Are you also seduced? Hath
any one of the rulers believed in him, or of the
49 Pharisees? But this multitude, that knoweth not the
50 law, are accursed. Nicodemus said to them, he that
51 came to him by night, who was one of them: Doth
our law judge any man, unless it first hear him, and
52 know what he doeth? They answered, and said to
him: Art thou also a Galilean? Search the Scriptures,
53 and see that out of Galilee a prophet riseth not. And
every man returned to his own house.

CHAP. VIII. } And Jesus went to mount Olivet. And early
v. 1–2. } in the morning, he came again into the temple: and all the people came to him, and sitting he
3 taught them. And the Scribes and Pharisees bring to
him a woman taken in adultery; and they set her in
4 the midst, And said to him: Master this woman was
5 even now taken in adultery. Now Moses in the law
commanded us to stone such a one. But what sayest
6 thou? And this they said, tempting him, that they
might accuse him. But Jesus, stooping down, wrote
7 with his finger on the ground. And when they continued asking him, he lifted up himself and said to
them: He that is without sin among you, let him first
8 cast a stone at her. And again he stooped down, and
9 wrote on the ground. But they, hearing *this*, went out
one by one, beginning from the eldest: and Jesus
alone remained and the woman standing in the midst.
10 Then Jesus lifting up himself, said to her: Woman,
where are they that accused thee? Hath no man
11 condemned thee? And she said: No man, Lord.
And Jesus said: Neither will I condemn thee. Go,
12 and now sin no more. And again Jesus spoke to
them, saying: I am the light of the world: he that
followeth me, walketh not in darkness, but shall have
13 the light of life. The Pharisees, therefore, said to
him: Thou givest testimony of thyself: thy testimony

14 is not true. Jesus answered, and said to them:
Although I give testimony of myself, my testimony is
true: for I know whence I came, and whither I go:
but you know not whence I come, or whither I go.
15 You judge according to the flesh: I judge not any
16 man: And if I do judge, my judgment is true, because I am not alone; but I and he that sent me, the
17 Father. And in your law it is written, that the testi-
18 mony of two men is true. I am one that give testimony of myself: and the Father that sent me, giveth
19 testimony of me. They said therefore to him: Where
is thy Father? Jesus answered: Neither me do you
know, nor my Father: If you did know me, you
20 would know my Father also. These words Jesus
spoke in the treasury, teaching in the temple: and
no man laid hands on him, because his hour was not
21 yet come. Then Jesus said to them again: I go my
way, and you shall seek me, and you shall die in
22 your sin. Whither I go, you cannot come. The
Jews, therefore, said: Will he kill himself, because
23 he said: Whither I go, you cannot come? And he
said to them: You are from beneath: I am from
above. You are of this world: I am not of this
24 world. Therefore I said to you, that you shall die
in your sins: for if you believe not that I am he,
25 you shall die in your sin. They said, therefore, to
him: Who art thou? Jesus said to them: The
26 beginning, who also speak to you. I have many
things to speak, and to judge of you. But he that
sent me is true: and the things I have heard from
27 him, the same I speak in the world. Now they did
28 not know that he said God was his Father. Jesus,
therefore, said to them: When you shall have lifted
up the Son of man, then shall you know that I am
he, and that I do nothing of myself; but as the Fa-
29 ther hath taught me, I speak these things; And
he that sent me, is with me; and he hath not left
me alone: for I do always the things that please him.
30 When he spoke these things, many believed in him.
31 Then Jesus said to those Jews that believed him:
If you continue in my word, you shall be my disci-
32 ples indeed: And you shall know the truth, and the

33 truth shall make you free. They answered him:
We are the seed of Abraham; and we have never
been slaves to any man: how sayest thou, You shall
34 be free? Jusus answered them: Amen, amen I say
unto you: That whosoever committeth sin, is the
35 servant of sin. Now the servant abideth not in the
36 house for ever: but the Son abideth for ever. If,
therefore, the Son shall make you free, you shall be
37 free indeed. I know that you are the children of
Abraham: but you seek to kill me, because my word
38 hath no place in you. I speak that which I have
seen with my Father: and you do the things that
39 you have seen with your father. They answered and
said to him: Abraham is our father. Jesus saith
to them: If you be the children of Abraham, do the
40 works of Abraham. But now you seek to kill me, a
man who have spoken the truth to you, which I have
41 heard from God: this Abraham did not. You do
the deeds of your father. They said then to him:
We are not born of fornication: we have one Father,
42 God. But Jesus said to them: If God were your
Father, verily you would love me. For I proceeded
and came from God: for I came not of myself, but
43 he sent me. Why do you not know my speech?
44 Because you cannot hear my word. You are of
your father, the devil; and the desires of your father you will do. He was a murderer from the beginning, and he abode not in the truth: because truth
is not in him. When he speaketh a lie, he speaketh
of his own: for he is a liar, and the father thereof.
45–46 But if I say the truth, you believe me not. Which
of you shall convince me of sin? If I say the truth
47 to you, why do you not believe me? He that is of
God, heareth the words of God. Therefore you hear
48 them not, because you are not of God. The Jews,
therefore, answered, and said to him: Do we not
say well that thou art a Samaritan, and hast a devil?
49 Jesus answered: I am not a devil: but I honour
50 my Father, and you have dishonoured me. But I
seek not my own glory: there is one that seeketh and
51 judgeth. Amen, amen I say unto you, if any man
52 keep my word, he shall not see death for ever. The

Jews, therefore, said: Now we know that thou hast
a devil. Abraham is dead, and the prophets: and
thou sayest: If any man keep my word, he shall not
53 taste death for ever. Art thou greater than our father
Abraham, who is dead? and the prophets are dead.
54 Whom dost thou make thyself? Jesus answered: If
I glorify myself, my glory is nothing: it is my Father
that glorifieth me, of whom you say that he is your
55 God. And you have not known him: but I know
him: and if I should say that I know him not, I
should be like to you, a liar. But I know him and
56 keep his word. Abraham your father rejoiced that
that he might see my day: he saw it, and was glad.
57 The Jews then said to him: Thou art not yet fifty
58 years old; and hast thou seen Abraham? Jesus said
to them: Amen, amen I say to you, before Abra-
59 ham was made, I am. Then they took up stones to
cast at him: but Jesus hid himself, and went out of
the temple.

CHAP. IX. v. 1–2. And Jesus passed by a man that was blind
from his birth: And his disciples asked him:
Rabbi, who hath sinned, this man or his parents, that
3 he should be born blind? Jesus answered: Neither
hath this man sinned, nor his parents; but that the
4 works of God should be made manifest in him. I
must work the works of him that sent me, whilst it is
5 day: the night cometh, when no man can work. As
long as I am in the world, I am the light of the world.
6 When he had said these things, he spat on the ground,
and made clay of the spittle, and spread the clay
7 upon his eyes; And said to him: Go, wash in the
pool of Siloe, (which is interpreted, Sent.) He went
8 therefore, and washed; and he came seeing. The
neighbours, therefore, and they who had seen him before that he was a beggar, said: Is not this he that
9 sat, and begged? Some said: This is he. And
others, No, but he is like him. But he said: I am
10 he. They said, therefore, to him: How were thy
11 eyes opened. He answered: That man who is called
Jesus, made clay, and anointed my eyes, and said
to me: Go to the pool of Siloe, and wash. And I

12 went, I washed, and I see. And they said to him:
13 Where is he? He saith: I know not. They bring
14 him that had been blind, to the Pharisees. Now it
was the sabbath, when Jesus made the clay, and
15 opened his eyes. Again, therefore, the Pharisees
asked him how he had received his sight. But he
said to them: He put clay upon my eyes, and I
16 washed, and I see. Some, therefore, of the Pharisees said: This man is not of God, who keepeth not
the sabbath. But others said: How can a man that
is a sinner do such miracles? And there was a divi-
17 sion among them. They said therefore, to the blind
man again: What sayest thou of him, that hath
opened thy eyes? And he said: He is a prophet.
18 The Jews then did not believe concerning him, that
he had been blind, and had received his sight, until
they called the parents of him that had received
19 his sight; And asked them, saying: Is this your
son, who you say was born blind? How then doth
20 he now see? His parents answered them, and said:
We know that this is our son, and that he was born
21 blind: But how he now seeth we know not: or
who hath opened his eyes, we know not: ask himself:
22 he is of age; let him speak for himself. These things
his parents said, because they feared the Jews: for
the Jews had already agreed among themselves, that
if any man should confess him to be Christ, he should
23 be put out of the synagogue. Therefore did his pa-
24 rents say: He is of age; ask himself. They, therefore, called the man again that had been blind, and
said to him: Give glory to God. We know that
25 this man is a sinner. He said then to them: If he be
a sinner, I know not: one thing I know; that whereas
26 I was blind, I now see. Then they said to him:
What did he to thee? How did he open thy eyes?
27 He answered them: I have told you already, and
you have heard: why would you hear it again?
28 will you also become his disciples? They reviled
him, therefore, and said: Be thou his disciple: but
29 we are the disciples of Moses. We know that God
spoke to Moses; but as to this man, we know not
30 from whence he is. The man answered, and said to

them: For in this is a wonderful thing, that you
know not from whence he is, and he hath opened my
31 eyes. Now we know that God doth not hear sin
ners: but if a man be a worshipper of God, a
32 doeth his will, him he heareth. From the beginni
of the world it hath not been heard, that any m
33 hath opened the eyes of one born blind. Unless thi
34 man were of God, he could not do any thing. They
answered, and said to him: Thou wast wholly born
in sins, and dost thou teach us? And they cast him
35 out. Jesus heard that they had cast him out: and
when he had found him, he said to him: Dost thou
36 believe in the Son of God? He answered, and said:
37 Who is he, Lord, that I may believe in him? And
Jesus said to him: Thou hast both seen him, and
38 it is he who talketh with thee. And he said: I be-
39 lieve, Lord. And falling down, he adored him. And
Jesus said: For judgment I am come into this
world: that they who see not, may see: and they
40 who see, may become blind. And some of the Pharisees, that were with him, heard: and they said to
41 him: Are we also blind? Jesus said to them: If
you were blind, you should not have sin: but now
you say: We see. Your sin remaineth.

CHAP. X. v. 1. Amen, amen I say to you: He that entereth
not by the door into the sheepfold, but climbeth
up another way, the same is a thief and a robber.
2 But he that entereth in by the door, is the shepherd
3 of the sheep: To whom the porter openeth; and the
sheep hear his voice; and he calleth his own sheep
4 by name, and leadeth them out. And when he hath
let out his own sheep, he goeth before them: and the
5 sheep follow him, because they know his voice. But
a stranger they follow not, but fly from him; because
6 they know not the voice of strangers. This parable
Jesus spoke to them. But they understood not what
7 he was speaking to them. Jesus, therefore, said to
them again: Amen, amen I say to you, I am the
8 door of the sheep. All they who came are thieves
9 and robbers: and the sheep heard them not. I am
the door. If any one enter by me, he shall be saved

and he shall go in, and go out, and shall find pas-
10 tures. The thief cometh not, but to steal, and to
kill, and to destroy. I am come that they may have
11 life, and may have it more abundantly. I am the
good shepherd. The good shepherd giveth his life
12 for his sheep: But the hireling, and he that is not
the shepherd, whose own sheep they are not, seeth the
wolf coming, and leaveth the sheep and flieth: and
13 the wolf snatcheth and scattereth the sheep. And the
hireling flieth, because he is a hireling: and he hath
14 no care for the sheep. I am the good shepherd; and
15 I know mine, and mine know me; As the Father
knoweth me, and I know the Father: and I lay
16 down my life for my sheep. And other sheep I have,
that are not of this fold: them also I must bring;
and they shall hear my voice: and there shall be
17 made one fold and one shepherd. Therefore doth
the Father love me: because I lay down my life,
18 that I may take it again. No man taketh it away
from me: but I lay it down of myself, and I have
power to lay it down: and I have power to take it
up again. This commandment I have received from
19 my Father. A dissension rose again among the Jews
20 for these words. And many of them said: He hath
21 a devil, and is mad: Why hear you him? Others
said: These are not the words of one that hath a
22 devil: Can a devil open the eyes of the blind? And
it was the feast of the dedication at Jerusalem: and
23 it was winter. And Jesus walked in the temple, in
24 Solomon's porch. The Jews, therefore, came round
about him, and said to him: How long dost thou
hold our souls in suspense: if thou be the Christ, tell
25 us plainly. Jesus answered them: I speak to you,
and you believe not: the works that I do in the name
26 of my Father, they give testimony of me: But you
27 do not believe, because you are not of my sheep. My
sheep hear my voice: and I know them, and they
28 follow me: And I give them life everlasting: and
they shall not perish for ever, and no man shall
29 snatch them out of my hand. That which my Father hath given me, is greater than all: and no one
30 can snatch *them* out of the hand of my Father. I

31 and the Father are one. The Jews then took up
32 stones to stone him. Jesus answered them: Many
good works I have shown to you from my Father:
33 for which of those works do you stone me? The Jews
answered him: For a good work we stone thee not,
but for blasphemy: and because that thou, being a
34 man, makest thyself God. Jesus answered them:
Is it not written in your law: I said, you are Gods?
35 If he called them Gods, to whom the word of God
was spoken, and the Scripture cannot be made void:
36 Do you say of him, whom the Father hath sanctified
and sent into the world: Thou blasphemest: be-
37 cause I said, I am the Son of God? If I do not
38 the works of my Father, believe me not. But if I
do, though you will not believe me, believe the works
that you may know and believe that the Father is
39 in me, and I in the Father. They sought, therefore,
40 to take him: and he escaped out of their hands. And
he went away again beyond the Jordan into that place
where John was baptizing first: and there he abode:
41 And many resorted to him: and they said: John in-
42 deed did no sign. But all things whatsoever John
said of this man were true. And many believed in
him.

CHAP. XI. v. 1. Now there was a certain man sick, *named* Lazarus, of Bethania, of the town of Mary and
2 of Martha her sister. (And Mary was she that anointed the Lord with ointment, and wiped his feet with
3 her hair: whose brother Lazarus was sick.) His
sisters therefore sent to him, saying: Lord, behold,
4 he whom thou lovest is sick. And Jesus hearing it,
said to them: This sickness is not unto death, but for
the glory of God: that the Son of God may be glori-
5 fied by it. Now Jesus loved Martha, and her sister
6 Mary, and Lazarus. When he had heard, therefore,
that he was sick, he still remained in the same place
7 two days. Then after that he said to his disciples:
8 Let us go into Judea again. The disciples say to
him: Rabbi, the Jews but just now sought to stone
9 thee: and goest thou thither again? Jesus answered:
Are there not twelve hours of the day? If a man

walk in the day, he stumbleth not, because he seeth
10 the light of this world: But if he walk in the night,
11 he stumbleth, because the light is not in him. These
things he said: and after that, he said to them: Lazarus our friend sleepeth: but I go that I may awake
12 him out of sleep. His disciples, therefore, said: Lord,
13 if he sleep, he shall do well. But Jesus spoke of his
death: and they thought he spoke of the repose of
14 sleep. Then, therefore, Jesus said to them plainly:
15 Lazarus is dead: And I am glad for your sake, that
I was not there, that you may believe: but let us go
16 to him. Then Thomas, who is called Didymus, said
to his fellow disciples: Let us also go, that we may
17 die with him. So Jesus came; and found that he
18 had been four days already in the grave. (Now Bethania was near Jerusalem, about fifteen furlongs off.)
19 And many of the Jews were come to Martha and
Mary, to comfort them concerning their brother.
20 Martha, therefore, as soon as she heard that Jesus
was come, went to meet him: but Mary sat at home.
21 And Martha said to Jesus: Lord if thou hadst been
22 here, my brother had not died: But now also I know
that whatsoever thou wilt ask of God, God will give
23 it thee. Jesus saith to her: Thy brother shall rise
24 again. Martha saith to him: I know that he shall
25 rise again in the resurrection at the last day. Jesus
said to her: I am the resurrection and the life: he
that believeth in me, although he be dead, shall live:
26 And every one that liveth, and believeth in me, shall
27 not die for ever. Believest thou this? She saith to
him: Yea, Lord, I have believed that thou art Christ
the Son of the living God, who art come into this
28 world. And when she had said these things, she
went and called her sister Mary secretly, saying:
29 The master is come, and calleth for thee. She, as
soon as she heard *this*, riseth quickly, and cometh to
30 him. For Jesus was not yet come into the town:
but he was still in that place where Martha had met
31 him. The Jews, therefore, who were with her in the
house, and comforted her, when they saw Mary that
she rose up speedily and went out, followed her, say-
32 ing: She goeth to the sepulchre to weep there. When

Mary, therefore, was come where Jesus was, seeing
him, she fell down at his feet, and saith to him: Lord,
if thou hadst been here, my brother had not died.
33 When Jesus, therefore, saw her weeping, and the
Jews that were come with her weeping, he groaned
34 in the spirit, and troubled himself, And said: Where
have you laid him? They say to him: Lord, come
35–36 and see. And Jesus wept. The Jews, therefore,
37 said: Behold how he loved him. But some of them
said: Could not he that opened the eyes of the man
born blind, have caused that this man should not die?
38 Jesus, therefore, again groaning in himself, cometh to
the sepulchre: Now it was a cave: and a stone was
39 laid over it. Jesus saith: Take away the stone.
Martha, the sister of him that was dead, saith unto
him: Lord, by this time he stinketh; for he is now
40 of four days. Jesus saith to her: Did I not say to
thee, that if thou wilt believe, thou shall see the glory
41 of God? They took, therefore, the stone away: And
Jesus, lifting up his eyes, said: Father, I give thee
42 thanks that thou hast heard me. And I knew that
thou hearest me always; but because of the people
who stand about, have I said it; that they may be-
43 lieve that thou hast sent me. When he had said
these things, he cried with a loud voice: Lazarus,
44 come forth. And presently he that had been dead
came forth, bound feet and hands with winding-bands,
and his face was bound about with a napkin. Jesus
45 said to them: Loose him, and let him go. Many,
therefore, of the Jews, who were come to Mary and
Martha, and had seen the things that Jesus did, be-
46 lieved in him. But some of them went to the Pharisees, and told them the things that Jesus had done.
47 The chief-priests, therefore, and the Pharisees gathered
a council, and said: What do we, for this man doeth
48 many miracles? If we let him alone so all men will
believe in him: and the Romans will come, and take
49 away our place and nation. But one of them, named
Caiphas, being the high-priest of that year, said to
50 them: You know nothing at all. Neither do you
consider that it is expedient for you that one man
should die for the people, and that the whole nation

51 perish not. And this he spoke not of himself: but
being the high-priest of that year, he prophesied that
52 Jesus should die for the nation; And not only for
the nation, but to gather together in one the children
53 of God, that were dispersed. From that day, there-
54 fore, they devised to put him to death. Wherefore
Jesus walked no more openly among the Jews: but
he went into a country near the desert, unto a city
that is called Ephrem: and there he abode with his
55 disciples. And the pasch of the Jews was at hand:
and many from the country went up to Jerusalem be-
56 fore the pasch, to purify themselves. They sought,
therefore, for Jesus: and they discoursed one with
another, standing in the temple: What think you,
that he is not come to the festival day? And the
chief-priests and the Pharisees had given a commandment, that if any man knew where he was, he should
tell, that they might apprehend him.

CHAP. XII. v. 1. Now six days before the pasch, Jesus came
to Bethania, where Lazarus had been dead,
2 whom Jesus raised to life. And they made him a
supper there: and Martha served: but Lazarus was
3 one of them that were at table with him. Mary,
therefore, took a pound of ointment of right spikenard,
of great value, and anointed the feet of Jesus, and
wiped his feet with her hair: and the house was filled
4 with the odour of the ointment. Then one of his
disciples, Judas Iscariot, he that was about to betray
5 him, said: Why was not this ointment sold for three
6 hundred pence, and given to the poor? Now he said
this, not because he cared for the poor, but because
he was a thief, and having the purse, carried what
7 was put therein. But Jesus said: Let her alone,
that she may keep it against the day of my burial.
8 For the poor you have always with you: but me you
9 have not always. A great multitude, therefore, of the
Jews knew that he was there: and they came, not for
Jesus's sake only, but that they might see Lazarus
10 whom he had raised from the dead. But the chief-
11 priests thought to kill Lazarus also: Because many
of the Jews by reason of him went away, and be-

12 lieved in Jesus. And on the next day a great multitude, that was come to the festival day, when they
13 had heard that Jesus was coming to Jerusalem, Took
branches of palm-trees, and went forth to meet him;
and cried: Hosanna, blessed is he, that cometh in
14 the name of the Lord, the king of Israel. And
Jesus found a young ass, and sat upon it, as it is
15 written: Fear not, daughter of Sion: behold, thy
16 king cometh sitting on the colt of an ass. These
things his disciples did not know at the first: but
when Jesus was glorified, then they remembered that
these things were written of him: and that they had
17 done these things to him. The multitude, therefore,
gave testimony, which was with him, when he called
Lazarus out of the grave, and raised him from the
18 dead. For which reason also the people came to
meet him: because they heard that he had done this
19 miracle. The Pharisees, therefore, said among themselves: Do you see that we prevail nothing? Behold
20 the whole world is gone after him. Now there were
certain Gentiles among them, that came up to adore
21 on the festival day. These, therefore, came to Philip,
who was of Bethsaida of Galilee, and desired him,
22 saying: Sir, we would willingly see Jesus. Philip
cometh and telleth Andrew: Again Andrew and
23 Philip told Jesus. But Jesus answered them, saying: The hour is come that the Son of man should
24 be glorified. Amen, amen I say to you, unless the
25 grain of wheat fall into the ground and die, Itself
remaineth alone. But if it die, it bringeth forth much
fruit. He that loveth his life shall lose it: and he
that hateth his life in this world, keepeth it unto life
26 everlasting. If any man minister to me, let him follow me: and where I am, there also shall my minister be. If any man minister to me, him will my
27 Father honour. Now is my soul troubled. And
what shall I say? Father, save me from this hour.
28 But for this cause I came unto this hour. Father,
glorify thy name. A voice therefore came from heaven: I have both glorified it, and I will glorify it
29 again. The multitude therefore that stood and heard
said that it thundered. Others said: An Angel spoke

30 to him. Jesus answered, and said: This voice came
31 not for me, but for your sake. Now is the judgment
of the world: now shall the prince of this world be
32 cast out. And I, if I be lifted up from the earth,
33 will draw all things to myself. (Now this he said,
34 signifying what death he should die.) The multitude answered him: We have heard out of the law
that Christ abideth for ever: and how sayest thou:
The Son of man must be lifted up? Who is this
35 Son of man? Jesus, therefore, said to them: Yet
a little while the light is among you. Walk whilst
you have the light, that the darkness overtake you
not: and he that walketh in darkness knoweth not
36 whither he goeth. Whilst you have the light, believe
in the light, that you may be the children of light.
These things Jesus spoke: and he went away, and
37 hid himself from them. And whereas he had done
so many miracles before them, they believed not in
38 him: That the saying of Isaias the prophet might be
fulfilled, which he said: Lord, who hath believed
our hearing? And to whom hath the arm of the
39 Lord been revealed? Therefore they could not be-
40 lieve; for Isaias said again: He hath blinded their
eyes, and hardened their hearts; that they should
not see with their eyes, nor understand with their
heart, and be converted, and I should heal them:
41 These things said Isaias, when he saw his glory, and
42 spoke of him. However many of the chief men also
believed in him: but because of the Pharisees they
did not confess it, that they might not be cast out of
43 the synagogue. For they loved the glory of men,
44 more than the glory of God. But Jesus cried out,
and said: He that believeth in me, doth not believe
45 in me, but in him that sent me. And he that seeth
46 me, seeth him that sent me. I the light am come
into the world; that whosoever believeth in me may
47 not remain in darkness. And if any man hear my
words, and keep them not: I do not judge him: for
I came not to judge the world, but to save the world.
48 He that despiseth me, and receiveth not my words,
hath one that judgeth him. The word that I have
spoken, the same shall judge him in the last day.

49 For I have not spoken of myself; but the Father
who sent me, he gave me command what I should
50 say, and what I should speak. And I know that his
commandment is life everlasting. The things, therefore, that I speak, even as the Father said unto me,
so do I speak.

CHAP. XIII. } Before the festival day of the pasch, Jesus,
v. 1. } knowing that his hour was come, that he
should pass out of this world to the Father; having
loved his own, who were in the world, he loved them
2 to the end. And when supper was done, the devil
having now put into the heart of Judas *the son* of
3 Simon the Iscariot, to betray him: Knowing that
the Father had given him all things into his hands,
4 and that he came from God, and goeth to God: He
riseth from supper, and layeth aside his garments:
5 and having taken a towel, he girded himself. After
that, he poureth water into a bason, and began to
wash the feet of the disciples, and to wipe them with
6 the towel, wherewith he was girded. He cometh,
therefore, to Simon Peter. And Peter saith to him:
7 Lord, dost thou wash my feet? Jesus answered, and
said to him: What I do thou knowest not now; but
8 thou shalt know hereafter. Peter saith to him: Thou
shalt never wash my feet. Jesus answered him: If
I wash thee not, thou shalt have no part with me.
9 Simon Peter saith to him: Lord, not only my feet,
10 but also my hands and my head. Jesus saith to him:
He that is washed, needeth not but to wash his feet,
but is clean wholly. And you are clean, but not all.
11 For he knew who he was that would betray him:
12 therefore he said: You are not all clean. Then after
he had washed their feet, and taken his garments,
having set down again, he said to them: Know you
13 what I have done to you? You call me Master, and
14 Lord: and you say well: for so I am. If I, then,
being Lord and Master, have washed your feet; you
15 also ought to wash one another's feet. For I have
given you an example, that as I have done to you, so
16 you do also. Amen, amen I say to you: The servant is not greater than his lord: neither is an apostle

17 greater than he that sent him. If you know these
18 things, you shall be blessed if you do them. I speak
not of you all: I know whom I have chosen: but
that the Scripture may be fulfilled: He that eateth
19 bread with me, shall lift up his heel against me. At
present I tell you before it come to pass: that when it
shall come to pass, you may believe, that I am *the*
20 *Messias*. Amen, amen I say to you, he that receiveth whomsoever I send, receiveth me: and he that
21 receiveth me, receiveth him that sent me. When
Jesus had said these things, he was troubled in spirit:
and he protested, and said: Amen, amen I say to
22 you: That one of you will betray me. The disciples, therefore, looked one upon another, doubting of
23 whom he spoke. Now there was leaning on Jesus's
24 bosom one of his disciples, whom Jesus loved. Simon
Peter, therefore, beckoned to him, and said to him:
25 Who is it of whom he speaketh? He, therefore, leaning on the breast of Jesus, saith to him: Lord, who
26 is it? Jesus answered: He it is, to whom I shall
reach bread dipped. And when he had dipped the
bread, he gave it to Judas Iscariot, *the son* of Simon.
27 And after the morsel, Satan entered into him. And
Jesus said to him: That which thou doest, do quickly.
28 Now no man at the table knew for what intent he said
29 this to him. For some thought, because Judas had
the purse, that Jesus had said to him: Buy those
things which we have need of for the festival day;
30 or that he should give something to the poor. He,
then, having received the morsel, went out immedi-
31 ately. And it was night. When, therefore, he was
gone out, Jesus said: Now is the Son of man glori-
32 fied: and God is glorified in him. If God be glorified
in him, God will also glorify him in himself: and
33 immediately will he glorify him. Little children, yet
a little while I am with you. You shall seek me:
and, as I said to the Jews: Whither I go, you cannot
34 come: so now I say to you. I give you a new commandment: That you love one another; as I have
35 loved you, that you also love one another. By this
shall all men know that you are my disciples, if you
36 have love one for another. Simon Peter saith to him:

Lord, whither goest thou? Jesus answered: Whither
I go, thou canst not follow me now; but thou shalt
37 follow me afterwards. Peter saith to him: Why
cannot I follow thee now? I will lay down my life
38 for thee. Jesus answered him: Wilt thou lay down
thy life for me? Amen, amen I say to thee, the cock
shall not crow, till thou deny me thrice.

CHAP. XIV. v. 1–2. } Let not your heart be troubled. You believe
in God; believe also in me. In my Father's
house there are many mansions. If not, I would have
told you; because I go to prepare a place for you.
3 And if I shall go and prepare a place for you, I will
come again, and will take you to myself; that where I
4 am, you also may be. And whither I go you know,
5 and the way you know. Thomas saith to him; Lord,
we know not whither thou goest; and how can we
6 know the way? Jesus saith to him: I am the way,
and the truth, and the life. No man cometh to the
7 Father, but by me. If you had known me, you
would surely have known my Father also: and from
henceforth you shall know him; and you have seen
8 him. Philip saith to him: Lord, show us the Father,
9 and it is enough for us. Jesus saith to him: Have I
been so long a time with you; and have you not
known me? Philip, he that seeth me, seeth the
Father also. How sayest thou, Show us the Father?
10 Do you not believe, that I am in the Father, and the
Father in me? The words that I speak to you, I
speak not of myself. But the Father who abideth
11 in me, he doeth the works. Believe you not that I
12 am in the Father, and the Father in me? Otherwise,
believe for the works themselves. Amen, amen I say
to you, he that believeth in me, the works that I do,
he shall do also, and greater than these shall he do:
13 because I go to the Father. And whatsoever you
shall ask the Father in my name, that will I do: that
14 the Father may be glorified in the Son. If you shall
15 ask me anything in my name, that I will do. If you
16 love me, keep my commandments. And I will ask
the Father, and he shall give you another Paraclete,
17 that he may abide with you for ever. The Spirit of

truth, whom the world cannot receive; because it
seeth him not, nor knoweth him: but you shall know
him; because he shall abide with you, and shall be
18 in you. I will not leave you orphans: I will come
19 to you. Yet a little while; and the world seeth me
no more. But you see me; because I live, and you
20 shall live. In that day you shall know that I am in
21 my Father, and you in me, and I in you. He that
hath my commandments, and keepeth them; he it is
that loveth me. And he that loveth me, shall be
loved by my Father: and I will love him, and will
22 manifest myself to him. Judas saith to him, not the
Iscariot: Lord, how is it that thou wilt manifest thy-
23 self to us, and not to the world? Jesus answered
and said to him: If any one love me he will keep
my word; and my Father will love him, and we will
24 come to him, and will make an abode with him: He
that loveth me not, keepeth not my words. And the
word which you have heard is not mine; but the Fa-
25 ther's who sent me. These things have I spoken to
26 you, remaining with you. But the Paraclete, the Holy
Ghost, whom the Father will send in my name, he
will teach you all things, and bring all things to your
27 mind, whatsoever I shall have said to you. Peace
I leave with you, my peace I give to you: not as the
world giveth, do I give to you. Let not your heart
28 be troubled, nor let it be afraid. You have heard
that I said to you: I go away, and I come again to
you. If you loved me, you would indeed be glad,
because I go to the Father: for the Father is greater
29 than I. And now I have told you before it come to
pass, that when it shall come to pass, you may believe.
30 Now I will not speak many things with you. For
the prince of this world cometh; and in me he hath
31 not any thing. But that the world may know that I
love the Father, and as the Father hath given me
commandment, so I do. Arise, let us go hence.

CHAP. XV. v. 1–2. I am the true vine; and my Father is the
husbandman. Every branch in me, that
beareth not fruit, he will take away: and every one
that beareth fruit, he will purge it, that it may bring

3 forth more fruit. Now you are clean by reason of
4 the word, which I have spoken to you. Remain in
me, and I in you. As the branch cannot bear fruit
of itself, unless it abide in the vine, so neither can
5 you, unless you abide in me. I am the vine; you
the branches; he that abideth in me, and I in him, the
same beareth much fruit: for without me you can do
6 nothing. If any one remaineth not in me, he shall
be cast forth as a branch, and shall wither, and they
shall gather him up, and cast him into the fire; and
7 he burneth. If you remain in me, and my words
remain in you; you shall ask whatever you will, and
8 it shall be done to you. In this is my Father glorified, that you bring forth very much fruit, and become
9 my disciples. As the Father hath loved me, I also
10 have loved you. Remain in my love. If you keep
my commandments, you will remain in my love; as I
also have kept my Father's commandments, and do
11 remain in his love. These things I have spoken to
you; that my joy may be in you, and your joy may
12 be filled. This is my commandment, that you love
13 one another, as I have loved you. Greater love than
this no man hath, that a man lay down his life for his
14 friends. You are my friends, if you do the things
15 that I command you. I will not now call you servants: for the servant knoweth not what his Lord
doeth. But I have called you friends; because all
things whatsoever I have heard from my Father, I
16 have made known to you. You have not chosen me:
but I have chosen you, and have appointed you, that
you should go, and should bring forth fruit, and your
fruit should remain; that whatsoever you shall ask of
17 the Father in my name, he may give it you. These
things I command you, that you love one another.
18 If the world hate you; know ye that it hated me be-
19 fore you. If you had been of the world, the world
would love its own: but because you are not of the
world, but I have chosen you out of the world, there-
20 fore the world hateth you. Remember my word
that I said to you: The servant is not greater than
his lord. If they have persecuted me, they will also
persecute you: if they have kept my word, they will

21 keep yours also. But all these things they will do to
you for my name's sake: because they know not him
22 that sent me. If I had not come, and spoken to them,
they would not have sin: but now they have no ex-
23 cuse for their sin. He that hateth me, hateth my
24 Father also. If I had not done among them the works
that no other man hath done, they would not have sin:
but now they have both seen and hated both me and
25 my Father. But that the word may be fulfilled which
is written in their law: They have hated me with-
26 out cause. But when the Paraclete shall come, whom
I will send you from the Father, the Spirit of truth,
who proceedeth from the Father, he shall give testi-
27 mony of me: And you shall give testimony, because
you are with me from the beginning.

CHAP. XVI. v. 1–2. These things have I spoken to you, that you
may not be scandalized. They will put
you out of the synagogues: yea, the hour cometh,
that whosoever killeth you, will think that he doeth
3 a service to God. And these things will they do to
you, because they have not known the Father, nor
4 me. But these things I have told you; that when
the hour of them shall come, you may remember that
5 I told you. But I told you not these things from the
beginning, because I was with you: and now I go to
him that sent me: and none of you asketh me:
6 Whither goest thou? But because I have spoken
these things to you, sorrow hath filled your heart.
7 But I tell you the truth; it is expedient for you that
I go: for if I go not, the Paraclete will not come to
8 you: but if I go, I will send him to you. And when
he shall come, he will convince the world of sin, and
9 of justice, and of judgment. Of sin indeed; because
10 they have not believed in me. And of justice; because I go to the Father; and you shall see me no
11 longer: And of judgment; because the prince of
12 this world is already judged. I have yet many things
13 to say to you: but you cannot bear them now. But
when he, the spirit of truth, shall come, he will teach
you all truth: for he shall not speak of himself: but
what things soever he shall hear, he shall speak: and

14 the things that are to come, he will show you. He
shall glorify me; because he shall receive of mine,
15 and will declare *it* to you. All things whatsoever the
Father hath, are mine. Therefore I said, that he
shall receive of mine, and will declare *it* to you.
16 A little while, and now you shall not see me: and
again a little while, and you shall see me: because I
17 go to the Father. Then some of his disciples said
one to another: What is this that he saith to us: A
little while, and you shall not see me: and again a
little while, and you shall see me: and because I go
18 to the Father? They said, therefore: What is this
that he saith, a little while? we know not what he
19 speaketh. And Jesus knew that they were desirous
to ask him: and he said to them: Of this do you
inquire among yourselves, because I said: A little
while, and you shall not see me: and again a little
20 while, and you shall see me. Amen, amen I say to
you, that you shall lament and weep; but the world
shall rejoice: and you shall be sorrowful; but your
21 sorrow shall be turned into joy. A woman when she
is in labour, hath sorrow, because her hour is come:
but when she hath brought forth the child, she remem-
bereth no more the anguish, for joy that a man is born
22 into the world. So also you now, indeed, have sorrow,
but I will see you again, and your heart shall rejoice:
23 and your joy no man shall take from you. And in
that day you shall not ask me any thing. Amen,
amen I say to you: If you ask the Father any thing
24 in my name, he will give it you. Hitherto you have
not asked any thing in my name. Ask, and you
25 shall receive; that your joy may be full. These
things have I spoken to you in proverbs. The hour
cometh when I will no more speak to you in proverbs,
26 but will show you plainly of the Father. In that day
you shall ask in my name: and I say not to you, that
27 I will ask the Father for you: For the Father himself loveth you; because you have loved me, and
28 have believed that I came forth from God. I came
forth from the Father, and am come into the world:
29 again I leave the world, and I go to the Father. His
disciples say to him: Behold, now thou speakest

30 plainly, and speakest no proverb. Now we know
that thou knowest all things, and that for thee it is
not needful that any man ask thee: in this we believe
31 that thou camest forth from God. Jesus answered
32 them: Now do you believe? Behold, the hour cometh, and is now come, that you shall be dispersed
every man to his own, and shall leave me alone:
and yet I am not alone; because the Father is with
33 me. These things have I spoken to you, that in me
you may have peace. In the world you shall have
distress: but have confidence; I have overcome the
world.

CHAP. XVII. } These things Jesus spoke: and lifting up
v. 1. } his eyes to heaven, he said: Father, the
hour is come; glorify thy Son, that thy Son may
2 glorify thee. As thou hast given him power over all
flesh, that he may give life everlasting to all whom
3 thou hast given him. And this is life everlasting;
that they may know thee, the only true God, and
4 Jesus Christ, whom thou hast sent. I have glorified
thee upon the earth: I have finished the work which
5 thou gavest me to do: And now glorify thou me, O
Father, with thyself, with the glory which I had with
6 thee, before the world was. I have manifested thy
name to the men whom thou hast given me out of the
world. Thine they were: and to me thou gavest
7 them: and they have kept thy word. Now they
have known that all things which thou hast given me
8 are from thee: Because the words which thou gavest
me, I have given to them: and they have received
them, and have known for certain that I came forth
from thee: and they have believed that thou didst
9 send me. I pray for them: I pray not for the world,
but for them whom thou hast given me; because they
10 are thine: And all mine are thine; and thine are
11 mine, and I am glorified in them. And now I am
no more in the world: and these are in the world,
and I come to thee. Holy Father, keep them in thy
name, whom thou hast given me: that they may be
12 one, as we also *are*. While I was with them I kept
them in thy name. Those whom thou gavest me I

have kept: and none of them hath perished, except
the son of perdition, that the scripture may be fulfilled.
13 And now I come to thee: and these things I speak
in the world, that they may have my joy filled in
14 themselves. I have given them thy word: and the
world hath hated them, because they are not of the
15 world: as I also am not of the world. I do not ask
that thou take them away out of the world, but that
16 thou preserve them from evil. They are not of the
17 world: as I also am not of the world. Sanctify them
18 in truth. Thy word is truth. As thou hast sent me
into the world, I also have sent them into the world.
19 And for them I do sanctify myself; that they also
20 may be sanctified in truth. And not for them only
do I pray, but for those also who through their word
21 shall believe in me: That they all may be one, as
thou, Father, in me, and I in thee, that they also
may be one in us; that the world may believe that
22 thou hast sent me. And the glory which thou hast
given me, I have given to them; that they may be
23 one, as we also are one. I in them, and thou in me;
that they may be made perfect in one; and that the
world may know that thou hast sent me, and hast
24 loved them, as thou hast also loved me. Father, I
will that where I am, they also whom thou hast given
me, may be with me; that they may see my glory,
which thou hast given me: because thou hast loved
25 me before the foundation of the world. Just Father,
the world hath not known thee: but I have known
thee: and these have known, that thou hast sent me.
26 And I have made known thy name to them, and will
make it known: that the love wherewith thou hast
loved me, may be in them, and I in them.

CHAP. XVIII. v. 1. } When Jesus had said these things, he
went forth with his disciples over the
brook Cedron, where there was a garden, into which
2 he entered with his disciples. Now Judas also, who
betrayed him, knew the place: because Jesus had
3 often resorted thither together with his disciples.
Judas, therefore, having received a band *of men*, and
servants, from the chief priests and the Pharisees,

cometh thither with lanterns and torches and weapons.
4 Jesus, therefore, knowing all things that were to come
upon him, went forward, and said to them: Whom
5 seek ye? They answered him: Jesus of Nazareth.
Jesus saith to them: I am he. And Judas, also, who
6 betrayed him, stood with them. As soon then as he
had said to them: I am he: they went backward,
7 and fell to the ground. Again therefore, he asked
them: Whom seek ye? And they said: Jesus of
8 Nazareth. Jesus answered, I have told you, that I
am he: if, therefore, you seek me, let these go their
9 way: That the word might be fulfilled which he
said: Of them whom thou hast given me, I have not
10 lost any one. Then Simon Peter, having a sword,
drew it; and struck the servant of the high-priest;
and cut off his right ear. And the name of the ser-
11 vant was Malchus. Then Jesus said to Peter: Put
up thy sword into the scabbard. The chalice which
12 my Father hath given me, shall I not drink it? Then
the band, and the tribune, and the servants of the
13 Jews, took Jesus and bound him: And they led
him away to Annas first; for he was father-in-law to
14 Caiphas, who was the high-priest of that year. Now
Caiphas was he, who had given the counsel to the
Jews, that it was expedient that one man should die
15 for the people. And Simon Peter followed Jesus;
and so did another disciple. And that disciple was
known to the high-priest, and went in with Jesus into
16 the court of the high-priest. But Peter stood at the
door without. Then the other disciple who was known
to the high-priest, went out, and spoke to the portress,
17 and brought in Peter. And the maid that was portress said to Peter: Art not thou also one of this
18 man's disciples? He saith: I am not. Now the servants and officers stood at a fire of coals, because it
was cold, and warmed themselves: and with them
19 was Peter also standing, and warmed himself. The
high-priest then asked Jesus of his disciples, and of
20 his doctrine. Jesus answered him: I have spoken
openly to the world: I have always taught in the
synagogue, and in the temple, whither all the Jews
21 resort: and in private I have spoken nothing. Why

askest thou me? ask them who have heard what I
have spoken to them: behold, they know what things
22 I have said. And when he had said these things,
one of the officers standing by gave Jesus a blow
23 saying: Answerest thou the high-priest so? Jesus
answered him: If I have spoken ill, give testimony
24 of the evil: but if well, why strikest thou me? And
Annas sent him bound to Caiphas the high-priest.
25 And Simon Peter was standing, and warming himself.
They said, therefore, to him: Art not thou also one
of his disciples? He denied it, and said: I am not.
26 One of the servants of the high-priest, a kinsman
to him whose ear Peter cut off, saith to him: Did
27 not I see thee in the garden with him? Then Peter
28 again denied: and immediately the cock crew. Then
they led Jesus from Caiphas to the governor's hall.
And it was morning: and they went not into the hall,
that they might not be defiled, but that they might eat
29 the pasch. Pilate, therefore, went out to them, and
said: What accusation bring you against this man?
30 They answered, and said to him: If he were not
a malefactor, we would not have delivered him up
31 to thee. Pilate then said to them: Take him you,
and judge him according to your law. The Jews
therefore said to him: It is not lawful for us to put
32 any one to death: That the word of Jesus might
be fulfilled, which he said, signifying what death he
33 should die. Pilate, therefore, went into the hall again,
and called Jesus, and said to him: Art thou the
34 king of the Jews? Jesus answered: Sayest thou
this thing of thyself, or have others told it thee of
35 me? Pilate answered: Am I a Jew? Thy nation
and the chief priests have delivered thee up to me.
36 What hast thou done? Jesus answered: My kingdom is not of this world. If my kingdom were of
this world, my servants would certainly strive that I
should not be delivered to the Jews: but now my
37 kingdom is not from hence. Pilate, therefore, said
to him: Art thou a king, then? Jesus answered:
Thou sayest that I am a king. For this was I born,
and for this came I into the world; that I should
give testimony to the truth: every one that is of the

38 truth heareth my voice. Pilate saith to him: What
is truth? And when he had said this, he went forth
again to the Jews; and saith to them: I find no
39 cause in him. But you have a custom that I should
release one unto you at the pasch: will you, therefore, that I release unto you the king of the Jews?
40 Then they all cried again, saying: Not this man,
but Barabbas. And Barabbas was a robber.

CHAP. XIX. v. 1–2. } Then, therefore, Pilate took Jesus, and
scourged him. And the soldiers, platting
a crown of thorns, put it upon his head: and about
3 him they put a purple garment. And they came to
him, and said: Hail, king of the Jews: and they
4 gave him blows. Pilate, therefore, went forth again,
and saith to them: Behold, I bring him forth to
you, that you may know that I find no cause in him.
5 (So Jesus came forth, bearing the crown of thorns,
and the purple garment.) And he saith to them:
6 Behold the man. When the chief-priests, therefore,
and the officers had seen him, they cried out, saying:
Crucify him, crucify him. Pilate saith to them: Take
him you, and crucify him: for I find no cause in him.
7 The Jews answered him: We have a law; and according to the law he ought to die; because he made
8 himself the Son of God. When Pilate, therefore,
9 had heard this saying, he feared the more. And he
entered into the hall again: and he said to Jesus:
Whence art thou? But Jesus gave him no answer.
10 Pilate therefore saith to him: Speakest thou not to
me? knowest thou not that I have power to crucify
11 thee, and I have power to release thee. Jesus answered: Thou shouldst not have any power against
me, unless it were given thee from above. Therefore,
he that hath delivered me to thee hath the greater
12 sin. And from thenceforth Pilate sought to release
him. But the Jews cried out, saying: If thou release this man, thou art not Cæsar's friend: for whosoever maketh himself a king, speaketh against Cæsar.
13 Now when Pilate had heard these words, he brought
Jesus forth; and sat down in the judgment-seat, in
the place that is called Lithostrotos, and in Hebrew

14 Gabbatha. And it was the parasceve of the pasch,
about the sixth hour: and he saith to the Jews: Be-
15 hold your king. But they cried out: Away with
him, away with him; crucify him. Pilate saith to
them: Shall I crucify your king? The chief-priests
16 answered: We have no king but Cæsar. Then,
therefore, he delivered him to them to be crucified.
17 And they took Jesus and led him forth. And bearing his own cross, he went forth to that place
which is called Calvary, but in Hebrew Golgotha:
18 Where they crucified him; and with him two others,
19 one on each side, and Jesus in the midst. And Pilate
wrote a title also: and he put it upon the cross. And
the writing was, JESUS OF NAZARETH, THE KING OF
20 THE JEWS. This title, therefore, many of the Jews
read: because the place where Jesus was crucified,
was near to the city: and it was written in Hebrew,
21 in Greek, and in Latin. Then the chief-priests of the
Jews said to Pilate: Write not, the king of the Jews;
22 but that he said, I am the king of the Jews. Pilate
answered: What I have written, I have written.
23 Then the soldiers, when they had crucified him, took
his garments (and they made four parts, to every soldier
a part) and also his coat. Now the coat was without
24 seam, woven from the top throughout. They said
then one to another: Let us not cut it; but let us
cast lots for it whose it shall be; that the Scripture
might be fulfilled, saying: They have parted my
garments among them; and upon my vesture they
have cast lot. And the soldiers, indeed, did these
25 things. Now there stood by the cross of Jesus, his
mother, and his mother's sister, Mary of Cleophas,
26 and Mary Magdalene. When Jesus, therefore, saw
his mother and the disciple standing, whom he loved,
27 he saith to his mother: Woman, behold thy son. After
that, he saith to the disciple: Behold thy mother.
And from that hour the disciple took her to his own.
28 Afterwards Jesus, knowing that all things were now
accomplished, that the Scripture might be fulfilled,
29 said: I thirst. Now there was a vessel set there,
full of vinegar. And they, putting a sponge full of
30 vinegar about hyssop, offered it to his mouth. When
Jesus, therefore, had taken the vinegar, he said: It

is consummated. And bowing his head, he gave up
31 the Ghost. Then the Jews, (because it was the parasceve) that the bodies might not remain upon the
cross on the sabbath day, (for that was a great sabbath-day) besought Pilate that their legs might be
32 broken, and that they might be taken away. The
soldiers, therefore, came: and they broke the legs of
the first, and of the other that was crucified with him.
33 But when they came to Jesus, and saw that he was
34 already dead, they did not break his legs: But one
of the soldiers opened his side with a spear: and im-
35 mediately there came out blood and water. And he
that saw it, gave testimony: and his testimony is true.
And he knoweth that he saith true; that you also
36 may believe. For these things were done, that the
Scripture might be fulfilled: You shall not break a
37 bone of him. And again another Scripture saith:
38 They shall look on him whom they pierced. And
after these things Joseph of Arimathea (because he
was a disciple of Jesus, but in private, for fear of the
Jews) besought Pilate that he might take away the
body of Jesus. And Pilate permitted him. He came,
39 therefore, and took away the body of Jesus. And
Nicodemus also came: he who at first came to Jesus
by night, bringing a mixture of myrrh and aloes,
40 about a hundred pounds. They took, therefore, the
body of Jesus, and bound it in linen-cloths with the
41 spices, as it is the custom with the Jews to bury. And
there was in the place where he was crucified, a garden; and in the garden a new sepulchre, wherein no
42 man had yet been laid. There, therefore, by reason
of the parasceve of the Jews, they laid Jesus, because the sepulchre was nigh at hand.

CHAP. XX. v. 1. } And on the first day of the week, Mary
Magdalene cometh in the morning, it being
yet dark to the sepulchre: and she saw the stone
2 taken away from the sepulchre. She ran, therefore,
and cometh to Simon Peter, and to the other disciple
whom Jesus loved; and saith to them: They have
taken away the Lord out of the sepulchre; and we
3 know not where they have laid him. Peter, therefore,

went out, and that other disciple; and they came to
4 the sepulchre. And they both did run together: and
that other disciple outran Peter, and came first to
5 the sepulchre. And when he stooped down, he saw
6 the linen-cloths lying; but yet he went not in. Then
cometh Simon Peter, following him, and went into
7 the sepulchre, and saw the linen-cloths lying; And
the napkin that had been about his head, not lying
with the linen-cloths, but apart, wrapt up into one
8 place. Then that other disciple also went in who
came first to the sepulchre: and he saw and believed.
9 For as yet they knew not the Scripture, that he must
10 rise again from the dead. So the disciples went away
11 again to their home. But Mary stood without at
the sepulchre, weeping: whilst she was then weeping, she stooped down, and looked into the sepulchre:
12 And she saw two Angels in white, sitting, one at the
head, and one at the feet, where the body of Jesus
13 had been laid. They say to her: Woman, why
weepest thou? She saith to them: Because they
have taken away my Lord, and I know not where
14 they have laid him. When she had said these words
she turned herself back, and saw Jesus standing: and
15 she knew not that it was Jesus. Jesus saith to her:
Woman, why weepest thou? whom seekest thou?
She, thinking that it was the gardener, saith to him:
Sir, if thou hast taken him away, tell me where thou
16 hast laid him; and I will take him away. Jesus
saith to her: Mary. She, turning, saith to him: Rab-
17 boni, (that is to say, Master.) Jesus saith to her:
Do not touch me; for I have not yet ascended to my
Father: but go to my brethren; and say to them:
I ascend to my Father and to your Father, to my
18 God and your God. Mary Magdalene cometh, tell-
ing the disciples: I have seen the Lord, and these
19 things he said to me. Now when it was late that
same day, being the first day of the week, and the
doors were shut, where the disciples were gathered
together, for fear of the Jews, Jesus came, and stood
in the midst, and said to them: Peace be to you.
20 And when he had said this, he showed them his hands
and his side. The disciples, therefore, were glad, when
21 they saw the Lord. And he said to them again:

Peace be to you. As the Father hath sent me, I
22 also send you. When he had said this he breathed
on them; and said to them: Receive ye the Holy
23 Ghost: Whose sins you shall forgive, they are forgiven them: and whose you shall retain, they are
24 retained. Now Thomas, one of the twelve, who is
called Didymous, was not with them when Jesus
25 came. The other disciples, therefore, said to him:
We have seen the Lord. But he said to them: Unless I shall see in his hands the print of the nails,
and put my finger in the place of the nails, and put
26 my hand into his side, I will not believe. And after
eight days, his disciples were again within, and Thomas
with them. Jesus cometh, the doors being shut, and
stood in the midst; and said: Peace be to you.
27 Then he saith to Thomas: Put in thy finger hither,
and see my hands, and bring hither thy hand, and
put it into my side: and be not incredulous, but faith-
28 ful. Thomas answered, and said to him: My Lord,
29 and my God. Jesus saith to him: Because thou
hast seen me, Thomas, thou hast believed: blessed
are they that have not seen, and have believed.
30 Many other signs also did Jesus in the sight of his
31 disciples, which are not written in this book. But
these are written, that you may believe that Jesus is
the Christ, the Son of God: and that believing, you
may have life in his name.

CHAP. XXI. v. 1. After this, Jesus showed himself again to
the disciples at the sea of Tiberias. And
2 he showed *himself* after this manner. There were
together Simon Peter, and Thomas who is called
Didymous, and Nathaniel who was of Cana in Galilee, and the sons of Zebedee, and two others of his
3 disciples. Simon Peter saith to them: I go a fishing.
They say to him: We also come with thee. And
they went forth, and entered into a ship: and that
4 night they caught nothing. But when the morning
was come, Jesus stood on the shore: yet the disciples
5 knew not that it was Jesus. And Jesus said to them:
Children, have you any meat? They answered him:
6 No. He saith to them: Cast the net on the right

side of the ship; and you shall find. They cast therefore: and now they were not able to draw it for t
7 multitude of fishes. That disciple, therefore, wh
Jesus loved, said to Peter: It is the Lord. Simon
Peter, when he heard that it was the Lord, girded
his coat about him (for he was naked,) and cast him-
8 self into the sea. But the other disciples came in the
ship (for they were not far from the land, but as it
were two hundred cubits,) drawing the net with fishes.
9 As soon, then, as they came to land, they saw hot
10 coals lying, and a fish laid thereon, and bread. Jesus
saith to them: Bring hither of the fishes that you
11 have now caught. Simon Peter went up, and drew
the net to land, full of great fishes, one hundred and
fifty-three. And although there were so many, the
12 net was not broken. Jesus saith to them: Come and
dine. And none of them who were at meat, durst
ask him: Who art thou? knowing that it was the
13 Lord. And Jesus cometh and taketh bread, and giv-
14 eth them, and fish in like manner. This is now the
third time that Jesus was manifested to his disciples,
15 after he was risen from the dead. When, therefore,
they had dined, Jesus saith to Simon Peter: Simon
son of John, lovest thou me more than these? He
saith to him: Yea, Lord, thou knowest that I love
16 thee. He saith to him: Feed my lambs. He saith
to him again: Simon *son* of John, lovest thou me?
He saith to him: Yea, Lord, thou knowest that
17 love thee. He saith to him: Feed my lambs. He
saith to him the third time: Simon *son* of John,
lovest thou me? Peter was grieved, because he said
to him the third time, Lovest thou me? And he
said to him: Lord, thou knowest all things: thou
knowest that I love thee. He said to him: Feed
18 my sheep. Amen, amen I say to thee: when th u
wast younger, thou didst gird thyself, and didst wa k
where thou wouldst: but when thou shalt be old, tho
shalt stretch forth thy hands; and another shall gird
19 thee, and lead thee whither thou wouldst not. And
this he said, signifying by what death he should glorify
God. And when he had said this, he saith to
20 him: Follow me. Peter turning about saw that
disciple, whom Jesus loved, following, who also leaned

on his breast at the supper, and said: Lord, who is
21 he that shall betray thee? Him, therefore, when
Peter had seen, he saith to Jesus: Lord, and what
22 shall this man *do?* Jesus saith to him: So I will
have him to remain till I come, what is it to thee?
23 follow thou me. This saying, therefore, went abroad
among the brethren, that that disciple dieth not. And
Jesus did not say to him: He dieth not: but so I
will have him to remain till I come, what is it to
24 thee? This is that disciple who giveth testimony
of these things, and hath written these things: and
25 we know that his testimony is true. But there are
also many other things, which Jesus did: which, if
they were written every one, the world itself, I think,
would not be able to contain the books that should be
written.

SELECTIONS FROM THE HOLY GOSPEL OF JESUS CHRIST ACCORDING TO SAINT MATTHEW.

CHAP. IV. v. 18. And Jesus walking by the sea of Galilee, saw
two brothers, Simon who is called Peter, and
Andrew his brother, casting a net into the sea (for
19 they were fishers.) And he saith to them: Come after
me, and I will make you become fishers of men.
20 And they immediately leaving their nets, followed
21 him. And going on from thence, he saw two other
brothers, James *the son* of Zebedee, and John his
brother, in a ship with Zebedee their father, mend-
22 ing their nets: and he called them. And they immediately leaving their nets and their father, followed
him.

CHAP. X. v. 2. Now the names of the twelve Apostles are
these: The first, Simon who is called Peter,
3 and Andrew his brother. James the son of Zebedee, and John his brother, Philip and Bartholomew,
Thomas and Matthew the publican, and James *the*
4 *son* of Alpheus, and Thaddeus. Simon Chananeus,
5 and Judas Iscariot, who also betrayed him. These
twelve Jesus sent; and commanded them, saying:

Go not into the way of the Gentiles; and into the
6 cities of the Samaritans enter not: But go rather
7 to the lost sheep of the house of Israel. And going
preach, saying: The kingdom of heaven is at hand.
8 Heal the sick, raise the dead, cleanse the lepers, cast
out devils: gratis you have received, gratis give.

CHAP. XIV. v. 22. } And forthwith Jesus obliged his disciples
to get up into the ship, and to go before
him over the water, while he sent the multitude
23 away. And when he had dismissed the multitude,
he went up into the mountain alone to pray. And
when the evening was come he was there alone.
24 But the ship in the midst of the sea was tossed
25 with the waves: for the wind was contrary. And
in the fourth watch of the night he came to them
26 walking upon the sea. And when they saw him
walking on the sea, they were troubled, saying: It
27 is an apparition. And they cried out for fear. And
immediately Jesus spoke to them, saying: Be of
28 good heart: It is I; be not afraid. And Peter
making answer, said: Lord, if it be thou, bid me
29 come to thee upon the waters. And he said: Come.
And Peter going down out of the ship, walked upon
30 the water to come to Jesus. But seeing the wind
strong, he was afraid: and when he began to sink,
31 he cried out, saying: Lord, save me. And immediately Jesus stretching forth his hand, took hold of
him and said to him: O thou of little faith, why
32 didst thou doubt? And when they were come into
33 the ship, the wind ceased. Then they that were in
the ship came and worshipped him, saying: Thou
art truly the Son of God.

CHAP. XVI. v. 13. } And Jesus came into the confines of Cesarea Philippi: and he asked his disciples,
saying: Whom do men say that the Son of man is?
14 And they said: Some *say that thou art* John the
Baptist, and others Elias, and others Jeremias, or
15 one of the prophets. He saith to them: But whom
16 do you say that I am? Simon Peter answering,
said: Thou art Christ, the Son of the living God.

17 And Jesus answering, said to him: Blessed art thou,
Simon Bar-jona: because flesh and blood hath not
revealed it to thee, but my Father who is in heaven.
18 And I say to thee: That thou art Peter, and upon
this rock I will build my church; and the gates of
19 hell shall not prevail against it. And I will give
to thee the keys of the kingdom of heaven: and
whatsoever thou shalt bind upon earth, it shall be
bound also in heaven: and whatsoever thou shalt
loose upon earth, it shall be loosed also in heaven.
20 Then he charged his disciples, that they should tell
21 no one that he was Jesus the Christ. From that
time forth Jesus began to show to his disciples, that
he must go to Jerusalem, and suffer many things
from the ancients and the scribes, and the chief
priests, and be put to death, and the third day rise
22 again. And Peter taking him began to rebuke him,
saying: Lord, be it far from thee; this shall not
23 be unto thee. But he, turning, said to Peter: Go
after me, Satan, thou art a scandal unto me: because thou dost not relish the things that are of
God, but the things that are of men.

CHAP. XVII. v 1. And after six days, Jesus taketh unto him
Peter and James, and John his brother,
and bringeth them up into a high mountain apart.
2 And he was transfigured before them. And his face
did shine as the sun: and his garments became as
3 white as snow. And, behold, there appeared to them
4 Moses and Elias, talking with him. Then Peter,
answering, said to Jesus: Lord, it is good for us to
be here: if thou wilt, let us make here three tabernacles, one for thee, and one for Moses, and one
5 for Elias. And as he was yet speaking, behold, a
bright cloud overshadowed them. And, behold, a
voice out of the cloud, saying: This is my beloved
6 Son, in whom I am well pleased: hear ye him. And
the disciples hearing, fell upon their face, and were
7 very much afraid. And Jesus came, and touched
them; and said to them: Arise, and be not afraid.
8 And when they lifted up their eyes, they saw no
9 man, but only Jesus. And as they came down from

the mountain, Jesus charged them, saying: Tell the
vision to no man, till the Son of man be risen
23 from the dead. And when they were come to Capharnaum, they that received the didrachma, came
to Peter, and said to him: Doth not your master
24 pay the didrachma? He said: Yes. And when he
was come into the house, Jesus prevented him, saying: What is thy opinion, Simon? Of whom do
the kings of the earth take tribute or custom? of
25 their own children, or of strangers? And he said:
Of strangers. Jesus said to him: Then the children
26 are free. But that we may not scandalize them,
go thou to the sea, and cast in a hook, and that fish
which shall first come up, take: and when thou
has opened its mouth, thou shalt find a stater: take
that, and give it to them for me and thee.

CHAP. XIX. v. 16. } And, behold, one came and said to him:
Good master, what good shall I do, that
17 I may have life everlasting? And he said to him:
Why askest thou me concerning good? One is good,
God. But if thou wilt enter into life, keep the
18 commandments. He saith to him: Which? And
Jesus said: Thou shalt do no murder: Thou shalt
not commit adultery: Thou shalt not steal: Thou
19 shalt not bear false witness: Honour thy father and
thy mother: and, Thou shalt love thy neighbour as
20 thyself. The young man saith to him: All these
have I kept from my youth: what is yet wanting
21 to me? Jesus saith to him: If thou wilt be perfect, go, sell what thou hast, and give to the poor;
and thou shalt have treasure in heaven: and come,
22 follow me. And when the young man had heard
this word, he went away sorrowfully: for he had
23 possessions. Then Jesus said to his disciples: Amen
I say to you, that a rich man shall hardly enter into
24 the kingdom of heaven. And again I say to you;
It is easier for a camel to pass through the eye of
a needle, than for a rich man to enter into the
25 kingdom of heaven. And when the disciples had
heard this, they wondered very much, saying: Who,
26 then, can be saved? And Jesus, beholding, said to

them: With men this is impossible: but with God
27 all things are possible. Then Peter, answering, said
to him: Behold, we have left all things, and have
28 followed thee: what, therefore, shall we have? And
Jesus said to them: Amen I say to you that you,
who have followed me, in the regeneration, when
the Son of man shall sit on the seat of his majesty,
you also shall sit on twelve seats judging the twelve
29 tribes of Israel. And every one that hath left house,
or brethren, or sisters, or father, or mother, or wife,
or children, or lands for my name's sake, shall receive a hundred-fold, and shall possess life everlast-
30 ing. But many that are first, shall be last: and
the last shall be first.

CHAP. XXVI. } And on the first day of the azymes the
v. 17. } disciples came to Jesus, saying: Where
wilt thou that we prepare for thee to eat the pasch?
18 But Jesus said: Go ye into the city to a certain
man, and say to him: The master saith: My time
is near at hand: I will keep the pasch at thy house
19 with my disciples. And the disciples did as Jesus
had appointed them: and they prepared the pasch.
20 Now when it was evening, he sat down with his
21 twelve disciples. And whilst they were eating, he
said: Amen I say to you, that one of you is about
22 to betray me. And they, being very much troubled,
23 began every one to say: Is it I, Lord? But he,
answering, said: He that dippeth his hand with
24 me in the dish, the same shall betray me. The
Son of man indeed goeth, as it is written of him:
but wo to that man by whom the Son of man shall
be betrayed. It were better for that man if he had
25 not been born. And Judas that betrayed him, answering, said: Is it I, Rabbi? He saith to him:
26 Thou hast said *it*. And whilst they were at supper, Jesus took bread, and blessed, and broke, and
gave to his disciples; and said: Take ye and eat:
27 This is my body. And taking the chalice, he gave
thanks; and gave to them, saying: Drink ye all
28 of this. For this is my blood of the new testament, which shall be shed for many for the remission

29 of sins. And I say to you: I will not drink from
henceforth of this fruit of the vine, until that day,
when I shall drink it new with you in the kingdom
30 of my Father. And when they had sung a hymn,
31 they went out to mount Olivet. Then Jesus saith
to them: All you shall be scandalized in me this
night. For it is written: I will strike the shepherd; and the sheep of the flock shall be dispersed.
32 But after I shall be risen again, I will go before
33 you into Galilee. And Peter answering, said to
him: Though all men shall be scandalized in thee,
34 I will never be scandalized. Jesus said to him:
Amen, I say to thee, that in this night before the
35 cock crow, thou wilt deny me thrice. Peter saith
to him: Though I should die with thee, I will
not deny thee. And in like manner said all the
36 disciples. Then Jesus came with them to a country
place which is called Gethsemani: and he said to
his disciples: Sit you here, till I go yonder and
37 pray. And taking with him Peter and the two
sons of Zebedee, he began to grow sorrowful, and
38 to be sad. Then he saith to them: My soul is
sorrowful even unto death: stay you here, and
39 watch with me. And going a little further, he fell
upon his face, praying, and saying: O my Father,
if it is possible, let this chalice pass from me.
40 Nevertheless, not as I will, but as thou *wilt.* And
he cometh to his disciples, and findeth them asleep:
and he saith to Peter: What! could you not watch
41 one hour with me? Watch ye, and pray, that ye
enter not into temptation. The spirit, indeed, is
42 willing, but the flesh weak. Again he went the
second time, and prayed, saying: O my Father,
if this chalice cannot pass away except I drink it,
43 thy will be done. And he cometh again, and findeth
44 them asleep: for their eyes were heavy. And leaving them, he went away again: and he prayed the
45 third time, saying the same words. Then he cometh to his disciples, and saith to them: Sleep on
now, and take your rest: behold, the hour is at
hand: and the Son of man shall be betrayed into
46 the hands of sinners. Rise, let us go: behold, he

47 is at hand that will betray me. As he yet spoke,
behold, Judas, one of the twelve, came, and with
him a great multitude with swords and clubs, sent
from the chief priests and ancients of the people.
48 And he that betrayed him, gave them a sign, saying: Whomsoever I shall kiss, that is he: hold
49 him fast. And forthwith coming to Jesus, he said:
50 Hail, Rabbi. And he kissed him. And Jesus said
to him: Friend, whereto art thou come? Then
they came up and laid hands on Jesus, and held
51 him. And behold, one of them that were with Jesus
stretching forth his hand, drew out his sword: and
striking the servant of the high-priest, cut off his
52 ear. Then Jesus saith to him: Put up again thy
sword into its place. For all that take the sword,
53 shall perish with the sword. Thinkest thou that I
cannot ask my Father, and he will give me pres-
54 ently more than twelve legions of angels? How then
shall the Scriptures be fulfilled, that so it must be
55 done? In that same hour Jesus said to the multitudes: You are come out as against a robber with
swords and clubs to apprehend me. I sat daily
with you teaching in the temple: and you laid not
56 hands on me. Now all this was done, that the
Scriptures of the prophets might be fulfilled. Then
57 the disciples all leaving him, fled away. But they,
holding Jesus, led him to Caiphas the high-priest,
where the scribes and the ancients were assembled:
58 But Peter followed him afar off, to the high-priest's
palace. And going in, he sat with the servants to
59 see the end. Now the chief priests and the whole
council sought false witness against Jesus, that they
60 might put him to death: And they found not,
though many false witnesses had come in. And
61 last of all there came in two false witnesses. And
they said: This man said: I am able to destroy
the temple of God, and in three days to rebuild it.
62 And the high-priest rising up, said to him: Answerest thou nothing to the things which these wit-
63 ness against thee? But Jesus held his peace. And
the high-priest said to him: I adjure thee by the
living God, that thou tell us if thou be the Christ

64 the Son of God. Jesus saith to him: Thou hast
said *it.* Nevertheless I say to you, Hereafter you
shall see the Son of man sitting on the right hand
of the power of God, and coming in the clouds of
65 heaven. Then the high-priest rent his garments,
saying: He hath blasphemed: what further need
have we of witnesses? Behold, now you have heard
66 the blasphemy: What think you? But they an-
67 swering, said: He is guilty of death. Then they
did spit in his face, and buffeted him: and others
68 struck his face with the palms of their hands, Saying: Prophesy unto us, O Christ; who is he that
69 struck thee? But Peter sat without in the palace:
and there came to him a servant-maid, saying: Thou
70 also wast with Jesus the Galilean. But he denied
before them all, saying: I know not what thou
71 sayest. And as he went out of the gate, another
maid saw him; and she saith to them that were
there: This man also was with Jesus of Nazareth.
72 And again he denied with an oath: I do not know
73 the man. And after a little while they that stood
by, came, and said to Peter: Surely thou also art
one of them; for even thy speech doth discover thee.
74 Then he began to curse and to swear that he knew
75 not the man. And immediately the cock crew. And
Peter remembered the word of Jesus which he had
said: Before the cock crow, thou wilt deny me
thrice. And going forth, he wept bitterly.

SELECTIONS FROM THE HOLY GOSPEL OF JESUS CHRIST ACCORDING TO ST. MARK.

CHAP. III. } And going up into a mountain, he called
v. 13. } unto him whom he would himself: and
14 they came to him. And he made that twelve should
be with him: and that he might send them to preach.
15 And he gave them power to heal sicknesses, and
16 to cast out devils. And to Simon he gave the
17 name of Peter: And James *the son* of Zebedee,
and John the brother of James, and he named
18 them Boanerges, which is, The sons of thunder: And
Andrew and Philip, and Bartholomew, and Matthew,

and Thomas, and James of Alpheus, and Thaddeus,
19 and Simon Cananeus, And Judas Iscariot, who also
betrayed him.

CHAP. XVI. } And when the sabbath was past, Mary
v. 1. } Magdalene and Mary *the mother* of James
and Salome, bought sweet spices, that coming they
2 might anoint Jesus. And very early in the morning the first day of the week, they come to the
3 sepulchre, the sun being now risen. And they said
one to another: Who shall roll us back the stone
4 from the door of the sepulchre? And looking, they
saw the stone rolled back. For it was very great.
5 And entering into the sepulchre, they saw a young
man sitting on the right side, clothed with a white
6 robe: and they were astonished. And he saith to
them: Be not affrighted; you seek Jesus of Nazareth, who was crucified: he is risen; he is not here;
7 behold the place where they laid him. But go tell
his disciples, and Peter, that he goeth before you
into Galilee: there you shall see him, as he told
8 you. But they going out, fled from the sepulchre;
for a trembling and fear had seized them: and they
said nothing to any man; for they were afraid.
9 But he rising early the first day of the week, appeared first to Mary Magdalene, out of whom he
10 had cast seven devils. She went, and told them
that had been with him, who were mourning and
11 weeping. And they hearing that he was alive, and
12 had been seen by her, did not believe. And after
that he appeared in another form to two of them
13 walking, as they were going into the country. And
they going told it to the rest: neither did they be-
14 lieve them. At length he appeared to the eleven
as they were at table: and he upbraided them with
their incredulity and hardness of heart; because they
did not believe them who had seen him after he
15 was risen again. And he said to them: Go ye
into the whole world, and preach the gospel to
16 every creature. He that believeth, and is baptized,
shall be saved: but he that believeth not, shall be
17 condemned. And these signs shall follow them that

believe: In my name they shall cast out devils:
18 they shall speak with new tongues: They shall
take up serpents: and if they shall drink any deadly
thing, it shall not hurt them: they shall lay their
19 hands upon the sick, and they shall recover. And
the Lord Jesus, after he had spoken to them, was
taken up into heaven, and sitteth on the right hand
20 of God. But they going forth preached everywhere;
the Lord co-operating with them, and confirming the
word with signs that followed.

SELECTIONS FROM THE HOLY GOSPEL OF JESUS CHRIST ACCORDING TO ST. LUKE.

CHAP. V. } And it came to pass that, when the multi-
v. 1. } tudes pressed upon him to hear the word
2 of God, he stood by the lake of Genesareth. And
he saw two ships standing by the lake: but the
fishermen were gone out of them, and were washing
3 their nets. And going up into one of the ships,
that was Simon's, he desired him to thrust out a
little from the land. And, sitting down, he taught
4 the multitudes out of the ship. Now when he had
ceased to speak, he said to Simon: Launch out
into the deep, and let down your nets for a draught.
5 And Simon answering, said to him: Master, we
have labored all the night, and have taken nothing;
6 but at thy word I will let down the net. And when
they had done this they enclosed a very great multi-
7 tude of fishes, and their net was breaking. And
they beckoned to their partners that were in the
other ship, that they should come and help them.
And they came, and filled both the ships, so that
8 they were almost sinking. Which when Simon
Peter saw, he fell down at Jesus's knees, saying:
Depart from me; for I am a sinful man, O Lord.
9 For he was wholly astonished, and all that were
with him, at the draught of the fishes which they
10 had taken: And so were also James and John,
the sons of Zebedee, who were Simon's partners.
And Jesus saith to Simon: Fear not: from hence-
11 forth thou shalt be taking men. And when they

had brought their ships to land, leaving all things,
they followed him.

CHAP. VI. } And it came to pass, in those days, that he
v. 12. } went out into a mountain to pray; and he
13 passed the whole night in the prayer of God. And
when it was day, he called his disciples: and he
chose twelve of them (whom also he named Apos-
14 tles:) Simon, whom he surnamed Peter, and Andrew his brother, James and John, Philip and Bar-
15 tholomew, Matthew and Thomas, James *the son* of
16 Alpheus, and Simon who is called Zelotes: And
Jude *the brother* of James, and Judas Iscariot, who
17 was the traitor. And, coming down with them, he
stood in an open plain, and the company of his
disciples, and a very great multitude of people from
all Judea and Jerusalem, and the sea-coast both of
18 Tyre and Sidon, Who had come to hear him, and
to be healed of their diseases. And they that were
19 troubled with unclean spirits were cured. And all
the multitude sought to touch him: for virtue went
out from him, and healed all.

CHAP. XII. } And when great multitudes stood about him,
v. 1. } so that they trod one upon another, he began
to say to his disciples: Beware ye of the leaven of the
2 Pharisees, which is hypocrisy. For there is nothing
covered that shall not be revealed: nor hidden, that
3 shall not be known. For whatsoever things you have
spoken in darkness, shall be published in the light:
and that which you have spoken in the ear in the
4 chambers, shall be proclaimed on the house-tops. And
I say to you, my friends: Be not afraid of them that
kill the body, and after that have no more that they
5 can do. But I will show you whom ye shall fear:
fear ye him who after he hath killed hath power to
6 cast into hell. Yea, I say to you, fear him. Are not
five sparrows sold for two farthings, and not one of
7 them is forgotten before God? But even the very
hairs of your head are all numbered. Fear not therefore: you are of more value than many sparrows.
8 And I say to you: whosoever shall confess me before

men, him shall the Son of man also confess before the
9 angels of God. But he that shall deny me before men,
10 shall be denied before the angels of God. And whosoever speaketh a word against the Son of man, it
shall be forgiven him: but to him that shall blaspheme
11 against the Holy Ghost, it shall not be forgiven. And
when they shall bring you into the synagogues, and
to magistrates, and powers, be not solicitous how or
12 what you shall answer, or what you shall say. For
the Holy Ghost shall teach you in the same hour
13 what you ought to say. And one of the multitude
said to him: Master, speak to my brother that he di-
14 vide the inheritance with me. But he said to him:
Man, who hath made me a judge or a divider over
15 you? And he said to them: Take heed and beware
of all covetousness: for a man's life doth not consist
in the abundance of things which he possesseth.
16 And he spoke a similitude to them, saying: The land
of a certain rich man brought forth plenty of fruits:
17 And he thought within himself, saying: What shall
I do, because I have not where to lay up together my
18 fruits? And he said: This will I do: I will pull down
my barns, and will build greater: and into them will
I gather all things that are grown to me, and all
19 my goods. And I will say to my soul: Soul, thou hast
much goods laid up for many years, take thy rest, eat,
20 drink, make good cheer. But God said to him: Thou
fool, this night do they require thy soul of thee: and
whose shall those things be, which thou has provided?
21 So is he that layeth up treasure for himself, and is not
22 rich towards God. And he said to his disciples:
Therefore I say to you: Be not solicitous for your life,
what you shall eat; nor for your body, what you shall
23 put on. The life is more than the food, and the body
24 is more than the raiment. Consider the ravens, for
they do not sow, nor do they reap, neither have they
store-house, nor barn, and God feedeth them. How
25 much are you more valuable than they? And which
of you by thinking can add to his stature one cubit?
26 If then you are not able to do even the least thing,
27 why are you solicitous for the rest? Consider the
lilies how they grow: they labour not, neither do they

spin. But I say to you not even Solomon in all his
28 glory was clothed like one of these. Now if God
clothe in this manner the grass that is to-day in the
field, and to-morrow is cast into the oven: how much
29 more you, O ye of little faith? And seek not you
what you shall eat, or what you shall drink: and be
30 not lifted up on high: For all these things do the
nations of the world seek after. But your Father
31 knoweth that you have need of these things. (But
seek ye first the kingdom of God and his justice: and
32 all these things shall be added unto you.) Fear not,
little flock, for it hath pleased your Father to give you
33 a kingdom. Sell what you possess, and give alms.
Make to yourself bags which grow not old, a treasure
in heaven which faileth not: where the thief ap-
34 proacheth not, nor the moth corrupteth. For where
35 your treasure is, there will your heart be also. Let
your loins be girded, and lamps burning in your
36 hands, And you yourselves like to men who wait for
their lord, when he shall return from the wedding:
that when he cometh, and knocketh, they may open to
37 him immediately. Blessed are those servants, whom
the Lord, when he cometh, shall find watching. Amen
I say to you, that he will gird himself, and make them
sit down to meat, and passing will minister to them.
38 And if he shall come in the second watch, or if he
shall come in the third watch, and find them so,
39 blessed are those servants. But this know ye, that if
a master of a family did know at what hour the thief
would come, he would surely watch, and would not
40 suffer his house to be broke open. Be you also ready:
for at what hour you think not, the Son of man will
41 come. And Peter said to him: Lord, dost thou speak
42 this parable to us, or likewise to all? And the Lord
said: Who (thinkest thou) is the faithful and wise
steward, whom his lord setteth over his family, to give
43 them their measure of wheat in due season? Blessed
is that servant, whom, when his lord shall come, he
44 shall find so doing. Verily I say to you, he will set
45 him over all that he possesseth. But if that servant
shall say in his heart, My lord is long a coming; and
shall begin to strike the men-servants and maid-ser-

46 vants, and to eat and to drink, and be drunk: The
lord of that servant will come in a day that he ex-
pecteth not, and at an hour that he knoweth not, and
shall separate him, and shall appoint him his portion
47 with unbelievers. And that servant who knew the
will of his lord, and hath not prepared, and did not
according to his will, shall be beaten with many
48 stripes. But he that knew not, and did things worthy
of stripes, shall be beaten with few stripes. And unto
whomsoever much is given, of him much shall be re-
quired: and to whom they have committed much, of
49 him they will demand the more. I am come to send
fire on the earth, and what will I but that it be kin-
50 dled? And I have a baptism, wherewith I am to be
baptized: and how am I straitened until it be accom-
51 plished? Think ye that I am come to give peace on
52 earth? I tell you no, but separation: For there shall
be from henceforth five in one house divided: three
53 against two, and two against three Shall be divided:
the father against the son, and the son against the
father, the mother against the daughter, and the daugh-
ter against the mother, the mother-in-law against her
daughter-in-law, and the daughter-in law against her
54 mother-in-law. And he said also to the multitudes:
When you see a cloud rising out of the west, presently
you say: A shower is coming: and so it happeneth:
55 And when *ye see* the south wind blow, you say: There
56 will be heat: and it cometh to pass. You hypocrites,
you know how to discern the face of the heavens, and
of the earth; but how is it that you do not discern this
57 time? And why even of yourselves do you not judge
58 that which is just? And when thou goest with thy
adversary to the prince, whilst thou art in the way en-
deavour to be delivered from him: lest perhaps he
draw thee to the judge, and the judge deliver thee to
59 the exactor, and the exactor cast thee into prison. I
say to thee, thou shalt not go out thence, until thou
payest the very last mite.

CHAP. XXII. } And the Lord said: Simon, Simon, be-
v. 31. } hold, Satan hath desired to have you,
32 that he may sift you as wheat: But I have prayed
for thee, that thy faith fail not: and thou being
33 once converted, confirm thy brethren. And he said
to him: Lord, I am ready to go with thee both
34 into prison, and to death. And he said: I say to
thee, Peter, the cock shall not crow this day, till
thou thrice deny that thou knowest me. And he
35 said to them: When I sent you without purse, and
36 scrip, and shoes, did you want anything? But they
said: Nothing. Then said he to them: But now
he that hath a purse, let him take it, and likewise
a scrip: and he that hath no sword, let him sell his
37 coat and buy one. For I say to you, that yet this,
that is written, must be fulfilled in me: And with
the wicked he was reputed: For the things con-
38 cerning me have an end. But they said: Lord, behold, here *are* two swords. And he said to them:
39 It is enough. And going out, he went, according to
his custom, to the mount of Olives. And his disci-
40 ples also followed him. And when he was come
to the place, he said to them: Pray, lest ye enter
41 into temptation. And he was withdrawn away from
them a stone's cast: and kneeling down, he prayed,
42 Saying: (Father, if thou wilt, remove this chalice
from me: nevertheless, not my will, but thine be
43 done. And there appeared to him an angel from
heaven, strengthening him.) And being in an agony,
44 he prayed the longer. And his sweat became as
45 drops of blood trickling down upon the ground. And
when he rose up from prayer, and was come to his
46 disciples, he found them sleeping for sorrow. And
he said to them: Why sleep you? arise, pray, lest
47 you enter into temptation. As he was yet speaking,
behold, a multitude: and he that was called Judas,
one of the twelve, went before them, and drew near
48 to Jesus, to kiss him. And Jesus said to him:
Judas, dost thou betray the Son of man with a kiss?
49 And they that were about him, seeing what would
follow, said to him: Lord, shall we strike with the
50 sword? And one of them struck the servant of

51 the high-priest, and cut off his right ear. But Jesus
answering, said: Suffer ye thus far. And when he
52 had touched his ear, he healed him. And Jesus
said to the chief-priests and magistrates of the temple, and the ancients that were come to him: Are
you come out, as it were against a thief, with swords
53 and clubs? When I was daily with you in the
temple, you did not stretch forth your hands against
me: but this is your hour, and the power of dark-
54 ness. Then apprehending him, they led him to the
high-priest's house: but Peter followed afar off.
55 And when they had kindled a fire in the midst of
the hall, and were sitting about it, Peter was in the
56 midst of them: Whom, when a certain servant-
maid had seen sitting at the light, and had looked
upon him, she said: This man was also with him.
57 But he denied him, saying: Woman, I know him
58 not. And after a little while, another seeing him,
said: Thou also art one of them. But Peter said:
59 O man, I am not. And about the space of one
hour after, another man affirmed, saying: Surely
this man was also with him: For he is also a
60 Galilean. And Peter said: Man, I know not what
thou sayest. And immediately, while he was yet
61 speaking, the cock crew. And the Lord turning,
looked on Peter. And Peter remembered the word
of the Lord, how he had said: Before the cock
62 crow, thou shalt deny me thrice. And Peter went
out, and wept bitterly.

SELECTIONS FROM THE ACTS OF THE APOSTLES.

CHAP. I. v. 1. The former treatise I have made, O Theophi-
lus, of all things which Jesus began to do
2 and to teach, Until the day on which, giving commands by the Holy Ghost to the apostles whom he
3 had chosen, he was taken up: To whom also he
showed himself alive, after his passion, by many
proofs; for forty days appearing to them, and speak-
4 ing of the kingdom of God. And eating with them,
he commanded them, that they should not depart
from Jerusalem, but should wait for the promise of
the Father, which, you have heard (saith he) by
5 my mouth. For John indeed baptized with water:
but you shall be baptized with the Holy Ghost, not
6 many days hence. They, therefore, who were come
together, asked him, saying: Lord, wilt thou at
7 this time restore again the kingdom to Israel? But
he said to them: It is not for you to know the
times or moments, which the Father hath put in
8 his own power. But you shall receive the power
of the Holy Ghost coming upon you, and you shall
be witnesses unto me in Jerusalem, and in all Judea,
and Samaria, and even to the uttermost part of
9 the earth. And when he had said these things,
while they looked on, he was raised up: and a
10 cloud received him out of their sight. And whilst
they were beholding him going up to heaven, behold, two men stood by them, in white garments,
11 Who also said: Ye men of Galilee, why stand
you looking up to heaven? This Jesus, who is

taken up from you into heaven, so shall he come as
12 you have seen him going into heaven. Then they
returned to Jerusalem, from the mount that is called
Olivet, which is near Jerusalem, within a sabbath-
13 day's journey. And when they had entered in, they
went up into an upper room, where there remained
Peter and John, James and Andrew, Philip and
Thomas, Bartholomew and Mathew, James of Al-
14 pheus, and Simon Zelotes, and Jude of James. All
these were persevering with one mind in prayer, with
the women, and Mary the mother of Jesus, and his
15 brethren. In those days Peter rising up in the midst
of the brethren, said: (Now the number of persons
16 together was about a hundred and twenty.) Men,
brethren, the Scripture must be fulfilled, which the
Holy Ghost foretold by the mouth of David, concerning Judas, who was the leader of them that
17 apprehended Jesus. Who was numbered with us,
18 and had obtained part of this ministry. And he
indeed hath possessed a field of the reward of iniquity; and, being hanged, burst asunder in the midst;
19 and all his bowels gushed out. And it became known
to all the inhabitants of Jerusalem: so that the
same field is called in their tongue, Haceldama, that
20 is, the field of blood. For it is written in the book
of Psalms: Let their habitation become desolate,
and let there be none to dwell therein: and let
21 another take his bishoprick. Wherefore, of these
men who have been with us, all the time that the
22 Lord Jesus came in and went out among us, Beginning from the baptism of John, until the day wherein
he was taken up from us, one of these must be
23 made a witness with us of his resurrection. And
they appointed two, Joseph, called Barsabas, who
24 was surnamed Justus, and Matthias. And praying,
they said: Thou, O Lord, who knowest the hearts
of all men, show which of these two thou hast chosen,
25 To take the place of this ministry, and apostleship,
from which Judas hath by transgression fallen, that
26 he might go to his own place. And they gave them
lots; and the lot fell upon Matthias: and he was
numbered with the eleven apostles.

CHAP. II. } And when the days of the Pentecost were
v. 1. } accomplished, they were all together in the
2 same place: And suddenly there came a sound from
heaven, as of a mighty wind coming: and it filled
3 the whole house where they were sitting. And there
appeared to them cloven tongues as it were of fire:
4 and it sat upon each of them: And they were all
filled with the Holy Ghost, and they began to speak
with divers tongues, according as the Holy Ghost gave
5 them to speak. Now there were dwelling at Jerusalem Jews, devout men, out of every nation under
6 heaven. And when this voice was made, the multitude came together, and was confounded in mind,
because that every one heard them speaking in his
7 own tongue. And they were all amazed, and wondered, saying: Behold, are not all these, who speak,
8 Galileans? And how have we every one heard our
9 own tongue wherein we were born? Parthians, and
Medes, and Elamites, and inhabitants of Mesopotamia,
10 Judea, and Capadocia, Pontus, and Asia, Phrygia, and
Pamphilia, Egypt, and the parts of Lybia about Cyrene,
11 and strangers of Rome, Jews also, and proselytes,
Cretes and Arabians: we have heard them speak in
12 our own tongues the wonderful works of God. And
they were all astonished, and wondered, saying one to
13 another: What meaneth this? But others mocking,
14 said: These men are full of new wine. But Peter,
standing up, with the eleven, lifted up his voice, and
spoke to them: Ye men of Judea, and all you that
dwell in Jerusalem, be this known to you, and with
15 your ears receive my words. For these are not drunk,
as you suppose, seeing it is but the third hour of the
16 day: But this is that which was spoken of by the
17 prophet Joel: And it shall come to pass, in the last
days, (saith the Lord) I will pour out of my spirit
upon all flesh: and your sons and your daughters shall
prophesy, and your young men shall see visions, and
18 your old men shall dream dreams. And upon my
servants, indeed, and upon my handmaids, will I pour
out in those days of my Spirit; and they shall proph-
19 esy: And I will show wonders in the heaven above,
and signs on the earth beneath; blood and fire, and

20 vapour of smoke. The sun shall be turned into darkness, and the moon into blood, before the great and
21 manifest day of the Lord cometh. And it shall come
to pass, that whosoever shall call upon the name of the
22 Lord, shall be saved. Ye men of Israel, hear these
words: Jesus of Nazareth, a man approved of God
among you, by miracles, and wonders, and signs, which
God did by him in the midst of you, as you also know:
23 This same being delivered up by the determinate
counsel and foreknowledge of God, you have crucified
24 and put to death by the hands of wicked men: Whom
God hath raised up, having loosed the sorrows of hell,
as it was impossible that he should be detained by it.
25 For David saith concerning him: I foresaw the Lord
always before my face: because he is at my right
26 hand, that I may not be moved: For this my heart
hath been glad, and my tongue hath rejoiced: more-
27 over, my flesh also shall rest in hope: Because thou
wilt not leave my soul in hell, nor suffer thy Holy One
28 to see corruption: Thou hast made known to me the
ways of life: Thou shalt make me full of joy with thy
29 countenance. Ye men, brethren, let me freely speak
to you of the patriarch David, that he died, and was
buried; and his sepulchre is with us to this present
30 day. Whereas, therefore, he was a prophet, and knew
that God had sworn to him with an oath, that of the
31 fruit of his loins one should sit upon his throne: Fore-
seeing he spoke of the resurrection of Christ, for
neither was he left in hell, neither did his flesh see cor-
32 ruption. This Jesus hath God raised up again,
33 whereof we all are witnesses. Being exalted, therefore, by the right hand of God, and having received
of the Father the promise of the Holy Ghost, he hath
34 poured forth this which you see and hear. For David
did not ascend into heaven: but he himself said: The
Lord said to my Lord, sit thou on my right hand,
35–36 Until I make thy enemies thy footstool. Therefore
let all the house of Israel know most assuredly, that
God hath made him Lord and Christ, this same Jesus,
37 whom you have crucified. Now when they had heard

these things, they had compunction in their heart; and
they said to Peter and to the rest of the apostles:
38 What shall we do, men brethren? But Peter to
them: Do penance, (said he) and be baptized every
one of you in the name of Jesus Christ, for the remission of your sins: and you shall receive the gift of
39 the Holy Ghost. For the promise is to you, and to
your children, and to all that are far off, whomsoever
40 the Lord our God shall call. And with a great many
other words did he testify and exhort them, saying:
41 Save yourselves from this perverse generation. They,
therefore, that received his word, were baptized: and
there were added to *them* in that day about three thou-
42 sand souls. And they were persevering in the doctrine
of the apostles, and in the communication of the break-
43 ing of bread, and in prayers. And fear came upon
every soul: and many wonders and signs were done
by the apostles in Jerusalem: and there was great fear
44 in all. And all they that believed were together, and
45 had all things common. They sold their possessions
and goods, and divided them to all, according as every
46 one had need. And continuing daily with one accord
in the temple, and breaking bread from house to house,
they took their meat with gladness and simplicity of
47 heart: Praising God together, and having favour
with all the people. And the Lord added daily to
their society such as should be saved.

CHAP. III. v. 1–2. } Now Peter and John went up to the temple,
at the ninth hour of prayer. And a certain
man, who was lame from his mother's womb, was carried: whom they laid daily at the gate of the temple,
which is called the Beautiful, that he might beg alms
3 of them that went into the temple. He, when he had
seen Peter and John about to go into the temple,
4 begged to receive an alms. But Peter, with John,
5 fixing his eyes upon him, said: Look upon us. And
he looked earnestly upon them, hoping that he should
6 receive something from them. But Peter said: Silver
and gold I have none: but what I have, I give thee:

in the name of Jesus Christ of Nazareth, rise up and
7 walk. And having taken him by the right hand, he
lifted him up, and forthwith his feet and soles became
8 firm. And he leaping up, stood, and walked; and
entered with them into the temple, walking, and leap-
9 ing, and praising God. And all the people saw him
10 walking and praising God. And they knew him, that
it was he who sat for alms at the Beautiful gate of the
temple: and they were filled with wonder and amaze-
11 ment at that which had happened to him. And as he
held Peter and John, all the people amazed ran to
12 them to the porch, which is called Solomon's. Which
Peter seeing, made answer to the people: Ye men of
Israel, why wonder you at this? or why look you upon
us as if by our strength or power we had made this
13 man to walk? The God of Abraham, and the God
of Isaac, and the God of Jacob, the God of our fathers,
hath glorified his Son Jesus, whom you indeed delivered up and denied before the face of Pilate, when he
14 judged he should be released. But you denied the
Holy and the just One, and desired a murderer to be
15 granted unto you. But the author of life you killed,
whom God hath raised from the dead, of which we
16 are witnesses. And his name, through the faith of his
name, hath made this man strong, whom you have seen
and known: and the faith which is by him hath given
17 this perfect soundness in the sight of you all. And
now, brethren, I know that you did it through igno-
18 rance, as also your rulers. But those things which
God had foretold by the mouths of all the prophets,
19 that his Christ should suffer, he hath so fulfilled. Be
penitent, therefore, and be converted, that your sins
20 may be blotted out: That, when the times of refresh-
ment shall come from the presence of the Lord, and
he shall send him who hath been preached unto you,
21 Jesus Christ, Whom heaven indeed must receive until
the times of the restitution of all things, which God
hath spoken by the mouth of his holy prophets from
22 the beginning of the world. For Moses indeed said:
A prophet shall the Lord your God raise up unto you

out of your brethren, like unto me: him you shall
hear, according to all things whatsoever he shall speak
23 to you. And it shall be, that every soul which will
not hear that prophet, shall be destroyed from among
24 the people. And all the prophets, from Samuel and
afterwards, that have spoken, have foretold these days.
25 You are the children of the prophets, and of the cove-
nant which God made to our fathers, saying to Abraham: And in thy seed shall all the families of the
26 earth be blessed. To you first God raising up his
son, sent him to bless you: that every one should convert himself from his wickedness.

CHAP. IV. v. 1. And when they were speaking to the people,
the priests and the officer of the temple and
2 the Sadducees came unto them; Being grieved that
they taught the people, and declared in Jesus the res-
3 urrection from the dead: And they laid hands on them,
and put them in custody, till the next day: for now it
4 was evening. But many of them who had heard the
word, believed: and the number of the men was made
5 five thousand. And it came to pass on the morrow,
that their rulers, and ancients, and scribes were gath-
6 ered together in Jerusalem: And Annas the high-
priest, and Caiphas, and John, and Alexander, and as
7 many as were of the priestly race: And setting them
in the midst, they asked: By what power or in what
8 name, have ye done this? Then Peter, filled with the
Holy Ghost, said to them: Ye rulers of the people
9 and ancients, hear: If we this day are examined concerning the good deed done to the infirm man, by what
10 means he hath been made whole; Be it known to you
all, and to all the people of Israel, that in the name of
our Lord Jesus Christ of Nazareth, whom you crucified,
whom God hath raised from the dead, even by him
11 doth this man stand here before you whole. This is
the stone which was rejected by you the builders;
12 which is become the head of the corner: Nor is there
salvation in any other. For there is no other name
under heaven given to men, whereby we must be

13 saved. Now they seeing the constancy of Peter and
John, knowing that they were illiterate and ignorant
men, they wondered: and they knew them, that they
14 had been with Jesus: Seeing also the man standi
with them, who had been healed, they could say n
15 ing against it. But they commanded them to go as
out of the council: and they conferred among the
16 selves, Saying: What shall we do to these men?
a miracle indeed hath been done by them, conspicuo
to all the inhabitants of Jerusalem: it is manifest, an
17 we cannot deny it. But that it may be no further
divulged among the people, let us threaten them, that
18 they speak no more in this name to any man. And
calling them, they charged them not to speak at all,
19 nor teach in the name of Jesus. But Peter and John
answering, said to them: If it be just in the sight of
20 God, to hear you rather than God, judge ye. For we
cannot but speak the things which we have seen and
21 heard. But they threatening them, sent them away;
not finding how they might punish them, because of
the people: for all men glorified what had been done,
22 in that which had come to pass. For the man was
above forty years old in whom that miraculous cure
23 had been wrought. And being let go, they came to
their own company, and related all that the chief
24 priests and ancients had said to them. Who when
they had heard *them*, with one accord lifted up their
voice to God, and said: Lord, thou art he that didst
make heaven and earth, the sea, and all things that are
25 in them: Who in the Holy Ghost, by the mouth of
our father David thy servant, hast said: Why have
the Gentiles raged, and the people devised vain things?
26 The kings of the earth stood up, and the princes assembled together against the Lord, and against his
27 Christ. For there were truly assembled in this city
against thy holy Son Jesus, whom thou hast anointed,
Herod, and Pontius Pilate, with the Gentiles and the
28 people of Israel, To do what thy hand and thy counsel
29 decreed to be done. And now, Lord, behold their
threatenings, and grant to thy servants, with all confi-

30 dence to speak thy word, In this, that thou stretch
forth thy hand to cures, and signs, and wonders, to be
31 done by the name of thy holy Son Jesus. And when
they had prayed, the place was shaken wherein they
were assembled: and they were all filled with the
Holy Ghost: and they spoke the word of God with
32 confidence. And the multitude of the believers had
but one heart and one soul: neither did any one of
them say, that, of the things which he possessed, any
thing was his own; but all things were common to
33 them. And with great power did the apostles give
testimony of the resurrection of Jesus Christ our
34 Lord: and great grace was in them all. For neither
was there any one among them that wanted. For as
many as were owners of lands or houses, sold them,
35 and brought the price of the things they sold, And
laid it down before the feet of the apostles. And dis-
tribution was made to every man according as he had
36 need. And Joseph, who by the apostles was surnamed
Barnabas, (which, being interpreted, is the son of con-
37 solation) a Levite, a Cyprian born, Having land, sold
it, and brought the price, and laid it at the feet of the
apostles.

CHAP. V. } But a certain man, named Ananias, with Sa-
v. 1–2. } phira his wife, sold a field, And by fraud
kept a part of the price of the field, his wife being
conscious of it; and bringing a certain part of it,
3 laid it at the feet of the apostles. But Peter said:
Ananias, why hath Satan tempted thy heart, that
thou shouldst lie to the Holy Ghost, and by fraud
4 keep part of the price of the field? Whilst it remained, did it not remain to thee? and being sold,
was it not in thy power? Why hast thou conceived
this thing in thy heart? Thou hast not lied to men,
5 but to God. And Ananias hearing these words, fell
down, and gave up the ghost. And great fear came
6 upon all that heard it. And the young men rising
up, removed him, and carrying him out, buried him.
7 And it came to pass, about the space of three hours
after, his wife also, not knowing what had happened,
8 came in. And Peter said to her: Tell me, woman,
whether you sold the field for so much? And she
9 said: Yea, for so much. And Peter *said* unto her:
Why have you agreed together to tempt the Spirit
of the Lord? Behold, the feet of those who have
buried thy husband, are at the door; and they shall
10 carry thee out. Immediately she fell down before
his feet, and gave up the ghost. And the young
men coming in, found her dead; and carried her
11 out, and buried her by her husband. And there
came great fear upon the whole Church, and upon all
12 that heard these things. And by the hands of the
apostles many signs and wonders were done among
the people. And they were all with one accord in
13 Solomon's porch. But of the rest no one durst join
himself to them: but the people magnified them.
14 And the multitude of men and women that believed
15 in the Lord was more increased. Insomuch that
they brought out the sick into the streets, and laid
them on beds and couches, that when Peter came,
his shadow at the least might overshadow any of them,
and they might be delivered from their infirmities.
16 And there came also together to Jerusalem a multitude out of the neighboring cities, bringing sick
persons, and such as were troubled with unclean

17 spirits: who were all healed. Then the high-priest
rising up, and all that were with him (which is the
heresy of the Sadducees,) were filled with indigna-
18 tion. And they laid hands on the apostles, and put
19 them in the common prison. But an angel of the
Lord by night opening the doors of the prison, and
20 leading them out, said: Go, and standing speak in
the temple to the people all the words of this life.
21 And they having heard this, entered early in the
morning into the temple, and taught. Now the high-
priest being arrived, and they that were with him,
assembled the council, and all the ancients of the
children of Israel; and sent to the prison to have
22 them brought. But when the officers came, and
having opened the prison, found them not, returning
23 back they told, Saying: The prison, indeed, we
found shut with all diligence, and the keepers standing before the doors: but opening it, we found no
24 man within. Now when the magistrate of the temple, and the chief-priest heard these words, they
25 were in doubt what was become of them. But a
certain man coming, told them: Behold, the men
whom you put in prison, are standing in the temple,
26 and teaching the people. Then went the magistrate
with the officers, and brought them without violence:
for they feared the people, lest they should be stoned.
27 And when they had brought them, they set them
before the council. And the high-priest spoke to
28 them, Saying: Commanding we commanded you,
that you should not teach in this name: and, behold,
you have filled Jerusalem with your doctrine: and
you have a mind to bring the blood of this man
29 upon us. Peter then answering, and the apostles,
said: We ought to obey God rather than men.
30 The God of our fathers hath raised up Jesus whom
31 you put to death, hanging him upon a tree. This
Prince and Saviour, God hath exalted with his
right hand, to give penitence to Israel, and remis-
32 sion of sins. And we are witnesses of these things,
and the Holy Ghost, whom God hath given to all
33 those that obey him. When they had heard these
things, they were cut to the heart; and they thought

34 to put them to death. But one in the council rising
up, a Pharisee, by name Gamaliel, a doctor of the
law, respected by all the people, commanded the
35 men to be put forth a little while. And he said to
them: Ye men of Israel, consider with yourselves,
36 what you are about to do with these men. For
before these days rose up Theodas, affirming himself
to be somebody, with whom joined a number of men
about four hundred; who was slain: and all who
believed in him were dispersed, and reduced to noth-
37 ing. After this man rose up Judas the Galilean in
the days of the enrolling, and drew away the people after him: he also perished: and all whosoever
38 consented to him were dispersed. And now, therefore, I say to you, refrain from these men, and let
them alone: for if this design, or work, be of men,
39 it will fall to nothing: But if it be of God, you
are not able to destroy it: lest perhaps you be found
40 to oppose God. And they consented to him. And
calling in the apostles, after they had been scourged,
they charged them not to speak at all in the name
41 of Jesus; and they dismissed them. And they indeed went from the presence of the council rejoicing,
that they were accounted worthy to suffer reproach
42 for the name of Jesus. And they ceased not every
day in the temple, and from house to house, to
teach and preach Christ Jesus.

CHAP. VIII. v. 14. Now when the apostles, who were in
Jerusalem, had heard that Samaria had
received the word of God, they sent to them Peter
15 and John: Who when they were come, prayed for
16 them, that they might receive the Holy Ghost: For
he was not yet come upon any one of them; but
they were only baptized in the name of the Lord
17 Jesus. Then they laid their hands upon them; and
18 they received the Holy Ghost. And when Simon
saw, that by the imposition of the hands of the
apostles the Holy Ghost was given, he offered them
19 money, Saying: Give me also this power, that on
whomsoever I shall lay hands, he may receive the
20 Holy Ghost. But Peter said to him: May thy

money perish with thee: because thou hast esteemed
21 the gift of God to be purchased with money. Thou
hast no part nor lot in this matter: for thy heart is
22 not right in the sight of God. Do penance, therefore, from this thy wickedness: and pray to God,
that perhaps this thought of thy heart may be for-
23 given thee: For I see thou art in the gall of
24 bitterness, and in the bonds of iniquity. Then Simon
answering, said: Pray you to the Lord for me,
that none of these things which you have said may
come upon me.

CHAP. IX. } And it came to pass, that Peter, as he passed
v. 32. } through visiting all, came to the saints who
33 dwelt at Lydda. And he found there a certain man
named Eneas, lying on his bed for eight years, who
34 was ill of the palsy. And Peter said to him: Eneas,
the Lord Jesus Christ healeth thee: arise, and make
35 thy bed. And immediately he arose. And all that
dwelt at Lydda and Saron saw him: and they were
36 converted to the Lord. And in Joppe there was a
certain disciple named Tabitha, which, being interpreted, is called Dorcas. This woman was full of
good works and alms-deeds, which she performed.
37 And it came to pass in those days, that she was sick,
and died. Whom when they had washed, they laid
38 her in an upper chamber. And Lydda being near
to Joppe, the disciples hearing that Peter was there,
sent two men to him with his request: Delay not
39 to come even to us. And Peter rising up, came
with them. And when he was arrived, they brought
him into the upper chamber: and all the widows
stood about him weeping, and showing him the coats
40 and garments which Dorcas had made them. And
having put them all out, Peter kneeling down, prayed,
and turning to the body, he said: Tabitha, arise.
And she opened her eyes; and having seen Peter,
41 sat up. And giving her his hand he raised her up.
And when he had called the saints and the widows,
42 he presented her alive. And it was made known
throughout all Joppe; and many believed in the

43 Lord. And it came to pass that he staid many days
in Joppe, with one Simon a tanner.

CHAP. X. } Now there was a certain man in Cesarea,
v. 1. } named Cornelius, a centurion of the band,
2 which is called the Italian, A religious man, and
one that feared God with all his house, who gave
much alms to the people, and prayed to God always:
3 He saw in a vision manifestly, about the ninth
hour of the day, an angel of God coming in to him,
4 and saying to him: Cornelius. And he beholding
him, being seized with fear, said: What is it, Lord?
And he said to him: Thy prayers and thy alms
have ascended for a memorial in the sight of God.
5 And now send men to Joppe, and call hither one
6 Simon, who is surnamed Peter: He lodgeth with
one Simon a tanner, whose house is by the sea side:
7 he shall tell thee what thou must do. And when
the angel who spoke to him was departed, he called
two of his household servants, and a soldier that
feared the Lord, of those who were under him:
8 To whom when he had related all, he sent them
9 to Joppe. And on the next day, whilst they were
going on their journey, and drawing near to the
city, Peter went up to the higher parts of the house
10 to pray, about the sixth hour. And being hungry,
he was desirous to taste *somewhat.* And as they
were preparing, there came upon him an ecstacy of
11 mind: And he saw heaven opened, and a certain
vessel descending, as it were a great sheet, let down
12 by the four corners from heaven to the earth, In
which were all manner of four-footed beasts, and
creeping things of the earth, and fowls of the air.
13 And there came a voice to him: Arise, Peter,
14 kill, and eat. But Peter said: Far be it from me,
Lord: for I have never eaten any common and un-
15 clean thing. And the voice *spoke* to him again the
second time: That which God hath purified, do not
16 thou call common. And this was done thrice: and
presently the vessel was taken up again into heaven.
17 Now whilst Peter was doubting within himself, what
the vision which he had seen should mean: behold,

the men who were sent by Cornelius, inquiring for
18 Simon's house, stood at the gate. And when they
had called, they asked if Simon who is surnamed
19 Peter, lodged there? And as Peter was thinking
on the vision, the Spirit said to him: Behold three
20 men seek thee. Arise therefore, go down, and go
with them, doubting nothing: for I have sent them.
21 Then Peter going down to the men, said: Behold,
I am he whom you seek: what is the cause for
22 which you are come? And they said, Cornelius,
the centurion, a just man and one that feareth God,
and that hath good testimony from all the nation of
the Jews, received an answer of a holy angel, to
send for thee into his house, and to hear words from
23 thee. Then bringing them in, he lodged them. And
the day following he arose, and went with them: and
some of the brethren from Joppe accompanied him.
24 And the day after he entered into Cesarea. Now
Cornelius was waiting for them, having called together
25 his kinsmen and special friends. And it came to
pass, when Peter was come in, Cornelius met him,
26 and falling down at his feet worshipped. But Peter
raised him up, saying: Rise, I myself also am a
27 man. And talking with him he went in, and found
28 many that were come together. And he said to
them: You know how abominable a thing it is for
a man that is a Jew, to keep company or to come
to one of another nation: but God hath showed to
29 me, not to call any man common or unclean. Wherefore making no doubt, I came when I was sent for.
I ask, therefore, for what cause you have sent for
30 me? And Cornelius said: Four days ago, until
this hour, I was praying in my house at the ninth
hour, and behold a man stood before me in white
31 apparel, and said: Cornelius, thy prayer is heard,
and thy alms are remembered in the sight of God.
32 Send therefore to Joppe, and call hither Simon, who
is surnamed Peter: he lodgeth in the house of Simon
33 a tanner by the sea side. Immediately therefore I
sent to thee: and thou hast done well in coming.
Now therefore all we are present in thy sight, to
hear all things whatsoever are commanded thee by

34 the Lord. Then Peter opening his mouth, said: In
truth I perceive that God is no respecter of persons:
35 But in every nation he that feareth him, and work-
36 eth justice, is acceptable to him. God send the
word to the children of Israel, preaching peace
37 through Jesus Christ: (he is Lord of all.) You
know the word which hath been published through
all Judea: for it began from Galilee, after the bap-
38 tism which John preached, Jesus of Nazareth: how
God anointed him with the Holy Ghost, and with
power, who went about doing good, and healing all
that were oppressed by the devil, for God was with
39 him. And we are witnesses of all things which he
did in the land of the Jews and in Jerusalem, whom
40 they killed, hanging him upon a tree. Him God
raised up the third day, and gave him to be made
41 manifest, Not to all the people, but to witnesses
pre-ordained of God, even to us, who eat and drank
42 with him after he arose again from the dead. And
he commanded us to preach to the people, and to
testify that it is he who hath been appointed by
God to be the Judge of the living and of the dead.
43 To him all the prophets give testimony, that through
his name all receive remission of sins, who believe
44 in him. While Peter was yet speaking these words
the Holy Ghost fell upon all them that were hear-
45 ing the word. And the faithful of the circumcision,
who had come with Peter, were astonished because
the grace of the Holy Ghost was also poured out
46 upon the Gentiles. For they heard them speaking
47 with tongues, and magnifying God. Then Peter
answered: Can any man forbid water, that these
should not be baptized, who have received the Holy
48 Ghost as well as we? And he commanded them
to be baptized in the name of the Lord Jesus Christ.
Then they entreated him to stay with them some
days.

CHAP. XI. v. 1. And the apostles and brethren who were in
Judea, heard that the Gentiles also had re-
2 ceived the word of God. And when Peter was
come up to Jerusalem, they who were of the circum-

3 cision disputed against him, Saying: Why didst thou
go in to men uncircumcised, and didst eat with them?
4 But Peter began and declared to them the *matter in*
5 order, saying: I was in the city of Joppe praying,
and I saw in an esctacy of mind a vision, a certain
vessel descending as it were a great sheet let down
from heaven by four corners, and it came even to
6 me: Into which looking I considered, and saw four-
footed creatures of the earth, and beasts and creep-
7 ing things, and fowls of the air: And I heard also
a voice, saying to me: Arise, Peter, kill, and eat.
8 And I said: By no means, Lord: for nothing common or unclean hath ever entered into my mouth.
9 And the voice answered the second time from heaven:
What God hath made clean call not thou common.
10 And this was done three times: and all were taken
11 up again into heaven. And behold, immediately
there were three men come to the house wherein I
12 was, sent to me from Cesarea. And the Spirit said
to me, that I should go with them, nothing doubting.
And these six brethren went with me also, and we
13 entered into the man's house. And he told us, how
he had seen an angel in his house, standing and
saying to him: Send to Joppe, and call hither
14 Simon, who is surnamed Peter, Who shall speak
to thee words, whereby thou and all thy house shall
15 be saved. And when he had begun to speak, the
Holy Ghost fell upon them, as upon us also in the
16 beginning. And I remembered the word of the
Lord, as he said: John indeed baptized with water,
17 but you shall be baptized with the Holy Ghost. If
then God gave to them the same grace, as to us also
who have believed in the Lord Jesus Christ: who
18 was I, that I could oppose God? When they had
heard these things, they held their peace: and glorified God, saying: God then hath also to the Gentiles given repentance unto life.

CHAP. XII. v. 1. } And at the same time Herod the king
stretched forth his hand to afflict some of
2 the church. And he killed James the brother of
3 John with a sword. And seeing that it pleased the

Jews, he proceeded further to take Peter also. (Now
4 it was in the days of the azymes.) Whom as soon
as he had apprehended, he cast into prison, deliver-
ing him to four quaternoins of soldiers to be kept,
intending after the pasch to bring him forth to the
5 people. Peter therefore was kept in prison. But
prayer was made without ceasing by the church to
6 God for him. And when Herod would have brought
him forth, that very night Peter was sleeping between two soldiers, bound with two chains: and the
7 guards before the door kept the prison. And behold,
an angel of the Lord stood by him: and a light
shined in the room: and he striking Peter on the
side, raised him up, saying: Arise quickly. And
8 the chains fell off from his hands. And the angel
said to him: Gird thyself, and put on thy sandals.
And he did so. And he said to him: Cast thy
9 garment about thee, and follow me. And going out
he followed him, and knew not that it was true,
which was done by the angel: but thought he saw a
10 vision. And having passed through the first and
the second ward, they came to the iron gate that
leadeth to the city, which of itself opened to them.
And going out, they passed on through one street:
11 and immediately the angel departed from him. And
Peter coming to himself, said: Now I know indeed, that the Lord hath sent his angel, and hath
delivered me out of the hand of Herod, and from
12 all the expectation of the people of the Jews. And
considering, he came to the house of Mary the mother
of John, who was surnamed Mark, where many were
13 assembled, and praying. And when he knocked at
the door of the gate, a damsel came to hearken,
14 named Rhode. And as soon as she knew Peter's
voice, she opened not the gate for joy, but running
15 in, she told that Peter stood before the gate. But
they said to her: Thou art mad. But she affirmed
that it was so. Then said they: It is his angel.
16 But Peter continued knocking. And when they had
17 opened, they saw him, and were astonished. But
he beckoning to them with his hand to hold their
peace, told how the Lord had brought him out of

prison, and he said: Tell these things to James
and to the brethren. And being gone out, he went
18 into another place. As soon as it was day, there was
no small confusion among the soldiers, what was
19 become of Peter. And when Herod had sought for
him, and found him not, having examined the keepers, he commanded they should be led away: and
going down from Judea to Cesarea, he stayed there.

CHAP. XV. v. 1. And some coming down from Judea, taught
the brethren: that unless you be circumcised after the manner of Moses, you cannot be
2 saved. And when Paul and Barnabas had no small
contest with them, they determined that Paul and
Barnabas, and certain others of the other side, should
go up to the apostles and priests to Jerusalem about
3 this question. They therefore being brought on their
way by the church, passed through Phenice and
Samaria, relating the conversion of the Gentiles:
4 and they caused great joy to all the brethren. And
when they were come to Jerusalem, they were received by the church, and by the apostles and ancients, declaring how great things God had done
5 with them. But there rose up some of the sect of
the Pharisees that believed, saying: They must be
circumcised, and be commanded to observe the law
6 of Moses. And the apostles and ancients came to-
7 gether to consider of this matter. And when there
was much disputing, Peter rising up, said to them:
Men brethren, you know that in former days God
made choice among us, that the Gentiles by my
mouth should hear the word of the Gospel, and be-
8 lieve. And God, who knoweth the hearts, gave
them testimony, giving to them the Holy Ghost as
9 well as to us. And made no difference between us
10 and them, purifying their hearts by faith. Now
therefore why tempt you God, to put a yoke upon
the necks of the disciples, which neither our fathers
11 nor we were able to bear? But by the grace of the
Lord Jesus Christ we believe to be saved, even as
12 they. And all the multitude held their peace: and
gave ear to Barnabas and Paul relating what great

signs and wonders God had wrought among the
13 Gentiles by them. And after they had held their
peace, James answered, saying: Men brethren, hear
14 me. Simon hath told in what manner God first
visited the Gentiles to take out of them a people
15 to his name. And to this agree the words of the
16 prophets, as it is written: After these things I will
return, and will rebuild the tabernacle of David,
which is fallen down, and I will rebuild the ruins
17 thereof, and I will set it up: That the rest of men
may seek after the Lord, and all nations upon whom
my name is invoked, saith the Lord who doeth these
18 things. To the Lord is known his own work from
19 the beginning of the world. Wherefore I judge that
they, who from among the Gentiles are converted to
20 God, are not to be disquieted. But that we write
to them, that they refrain themselves from the pollu-
tion of idols, and from fornication, and from things
21 strangled, and from blood. For Moses from ancient
times hath in every city them that preach him in
the synagogues, where he is read every sabbath.
22 Then it pleased the apostles and ancients, with the
whole church, to choose men of their own company,
and to send them to Antioch with Paul and Barnabas: Judas who was surnamed Barsabas, and Silas,
23 chief men among the brethren. Writing by their
hands. The apostles and ancients brethren to the
brethren of the Gentiles that are at Antioch and in
24 Syria and Cilicia, greeting: Forasmuch as we have
heard that some, who went out from us, have troubled
you with words, subverting your souls, to whom we
25 gave no commands: It hath seemed good to us
assembled together, to choose out men, and send
them to you with our dearly beloved Barnabas and
26 Paul. Men who have given their lives for the name
27 of our Lord Jesus Christ. We have sent therefore
Judas and Silas, who themselves also will by word
28 of mouth tell you the same things. For it hath
seemed good to the Holy Ghost, and to us, to lay
no further burden upon you than these necessary
29 things: That you abstain from things sacrificed to
idols, and from blood, and from things strangled,
and from fornication: from which things keeping
yourselves, you shall do well. Fare ye well.

SELECTIONS FROM THE EPISTLE OF ST. PAUL TO THE GALATIANS.

CHAP. I. v. 1. Paul, an apostle, not from men, neither by
man, but by Jesus Christ, and God the Fa-
2 ther, who raised him from the dead. And all the
brethren who are with me, to the churches of Galatia.
3 Grace be to you, and peace from God the Father
4 and from our Lord Jesus Christ, Who gave himself for our sins, that he might deliver us from this
present wicked world, according to the will of God
5 and our Father, To whom is glory for ever and
6 ever. Amen. I wonder that you are so soon removed, from him who called you to the grace of
7 Christ, to another gospel: Which is not another,
only there are some that trouble you, and would
8 pervert the gospel of Christ. But though we, or an
angel from heaven preach a gospel to you beside
that which we have preached to you, let him be
9 anathema. As we said before, so I say now again:
If any one preach to you a gospel besides that which
10 you have received, let him be anathema. For do I
now persuade men, or God? or do I seek to please
men? If I did yet please men, I should not be the
11 servant of Christ. For I give you to understand,
brethren, that the gospel which was preached by me
12 is not according to man. For neither did I receive
it from man, nor did I learn it, but by the revela-
13 tion of Jesus Christ. For you have heard of my
conversation in time past in the Jews' religion; how
that beyond measure I persecuted the church of
14 God, and laid it waste: And I made progress
in the Jews' religion, above many of my equals in
my own nation, being more abundantly zealous for
15 the traditions of my fathers. But when it pleased
him, who separated me from my mother's womb, and
16 called me by his grace, To reveal his Son in me,
that I might preach him among the Gentiles; imme-
mediately I condescended not to flesh and blood,
17 Neither went I to Jerusalem to the apostles who
were before me; but I went into Arabia: and again
18 I returned to Damascus: Then three years after,

I came to Jerusalem to see Peter, and stayed with
19 him fifteen days: But other of the apostles I saw
20 none, except James the brother of the Lord. Now
the things which I write to you, behold, before God
21 I lie not. Afterwards I came into the regions of
22 Syria and Cilicia. And I was unknown by face to
23 the churches of Judea, which were in Christ: But
they had heard only: He, that persecuted us in
times past, doth now preach the faith which once he
24 impugned: And they glorified God in me.

CHAP. II. v. 1. } Then fourteen years after, I went up again
to Jerusalem with Barnabas, taking Titus also
2 with me. And I went up according to revelation;
and communicated to them the gospel, which I
preach among the Gentiles, but apart to them who
seemed to be something; lest, perhaps, I should
3 run, or had run in vain. But neither Titus, who
was with me, being a Gentile, was compelled to be
4 circumcised: But because of false brethren unawares
brought in, who came in privately to spy our liberty,
which we have in Christ Jesus, that they might bring
5 us into bondage: To whom we yielded not by
subjection, no not for an hour, that the truth of the
6 gospel might continue with you: But of them who
seemed to be something, (what they were some time,
it is nothing to me; God accepteth not the person of
man) for to me they that seemed to be something,
7 added nothing. But on the contrary, when they had
seen that to me was committed the gospel of the
uncircumcision, as to Peter was that of the circum-
8 cision: (For he who wrought in Peter to the apostleship of the circumcision, wrought in me also among
9 the Gentiles:) And when they had known the
grace that was given to me, James and Cephas, and
John, who seemed to be pillars, gave to me and
Barnabas the right hands of fellowship; that we
should go to the Gentiles, and they to the circum-
10 cision: Only that we should be mindful of the poor,
11 which same thing also I was careful to do. But
when Cephas was come to Antioch, I withstood him
12 to the face, because he was blameable. For before

that some came from James, he did eat with the
Gentiles: but when they were come, he withdrew,
and separated himself, fearing those who were of the
13 circumcision. And to his dissimulation the rest of the
Jews consented; so that Barnabas also was led by
14 them into that dissimulation. But when I saw that
they walked not uprightly unto the truth of the
gospel, I said to Cephas, before them all: If thou,
being a Jew, livest after the manner of the Gentiles,
and not of the Jews, how dost thou compel the Gen-
15 tiles to follow the way of the Jews? We by nature
16 are Jews, and not of the Gentiles sinners. But
knowing that a man is not justified by the works of
the law, but by the faith of Jesus Christ; we also
believe in Christ Jesus, that we may be justified by
the faith of Christ, and not by the works of the law:
because by the works of the law no flesh shall be
17 justified. But if, while we seek to be justified in
Christ, we ourselves also are found sinners; is Christ
18 then the minister of sin? God forbid. For if I
build up again the things which I have destroyed,
19 I make myself a transgressor. For I, through the
law, am dead to the law, that I may live to God;
20 with Christ I am nailed to the cross. And I live,
now not I; but Christ liveth in me. And that I live
now in the flesh: I live in the faith of the Son
of God, who loveth me, and delivered himself for
21 me. I cast not away the grace of God. For if
justice be by the law, then Christ died in vain.

THE FIRST EPISTLE OF ST. PETER THE APOSTLE.

CHAP. I. v. 1. Peter, an apostle of Jesus Christ, to the
strangers dispersed through Pontus, Galatia,
2 Cappadocia, Asia, and Bithynia, elect, According
to the foreknowledge of God the Father unto the
sanctification of the Spirit, unto the obedience and
sprinkling of the blood of Jesus Christ: Grace
3 unto you, and peace be multiplied. Blessed be the
God and Father of our Lord Jesus Christ, who,
according to his great mercy, hath regenerated us

unto a lively hope, through the resurrection of Jesus
4 Christ from the dead, Unto an inheritance incorruptible, and undefiled, and that fadeth not, reserved in
5 heaven for you, Who, by the power of God, are
kept by faith unto salvation, ready to be revealed in
6 the last time. In which you shall greatly rejoice,
now if need be for a little time to be made sorrowful
7 in divers temptations: That the trial of your faith,
much more precious than gold (which is tried by the
fire) may be found unto praise, and glory, and hon-
8 our, at the appearing of Jesus Christ: Whom having
not seen you love: In whom also now, though you
see him not, you believe; and, believing, shall re-
9 joice with an unspeakable and glorified joy: Receiving the end of your faith, even the salvation of your
10 souls. Concerning which salvation the prophets have
inquired and diligently searched, who prophesied of
11 the grace to come in you: Searching into what time,
or manner of time, the Spirit of Christ should signify
in them; foretelling those sufferings that are in Christ,
12 and the glories that should follow: To whom it was
revealed, that not to themselves, but to you they
ministered those things, which are now declared to
you by those who have preached the gospel to you,
the Holy Ghost being sent down from heaven, on
13 whom the angels desire to look. Wherefore, having
the loins of your mind girded, being sober, hope
perfectly for that grace which is offered you at the
14 revelation of Jesus Christ: As children of obedience,
not conformed to the former desires of your ignorance:
15 But according to him who is holy, who hath called
16 you; be you also holy in all conversation: For it
is written: You shall be holy, because I am holy.
17 And if you invoke the Father, him who, without
respect of persons, judgeth according to every one's
work, converse in fear during the time of your
18 sojourning here: Knowing that you were not redeemed with corruptible gold or silver from your
vain conversation of the tradition of your fathers;
19 But with the precious blood of Christ, as of a lamb
20 unspotted and undefiled: Fore-known, indeed, before the foundation of the world, but manifested in

21 the last times for you. Who through him are faithful in God, who raised him from the dead, and gave
him glory, that your faith and hope might be in God:
22 Purifying your souls in the obedience of charity,
with a brotherly love from a sincere heart love one
23 another earnestly: Being born again not of corruptible seed, but incorruptible by the word of God,
24 who liveth and remaineth for ever. For all flesh is
as grass; and all the glory thereof as the flower of
the grass: the grass is withered; and the flower
25 thereof is fallen away. But the word of the Lord
endureth for ever: and this is the word which hath
been preached unto you.

CHAP. II. v. 1. } Wherefore, laying aside all malice, and all
guile, and dissimulations, and envies, and all
2 detractions, As new-born infants, desire the rational
milk without guile; that thereby you may grow unto
3 salvation: If yet you have tasted that the Lord is
4 sweet. To whom approaching the living stone, rejected indeed by men, but chosen and honoured of
5 God: Be you also as living stones built up, a spiritual
house, a holy priesthood, to offer up spiritual sacrifices,
6 acceptable to God by Jesus Christ. Wherefore, it is
contained in the Scripture: Behold, I lay in Sion
a chief corner-stone, elect precious: and he that
7 shall believe in him, shall not be confounded. To
you, therefore, that believe, honour: but to them that
believe not, the stone which the builders rejected,
8 the same is made the head of the corner: And a
stone of stumbling, and a rock of scandal to them,
who stumble at the word, neither do believe where-
9 unto also they are set. But you *are* a chosen generation, a royal priest-hood, a holy nation, a purchased
people: that you may declare his virtues, who hath
called you out of darkness into his admirable light.
10 Who in time past were not a people, but are now
the people of God: who had not obtained mercy,
11 but now have obtained mercy. Dearly beloved, I
beseech you, as strangers and pilgrims, to refrain
yourselves from carnal desires, which war against the
12 soul, Having your conversation good among the

Gentiles; that whereas they speak against you as
evil doers, considering you by *your* good works,
13 they may glorify God in the day of visitation. Be
ye subject, therefore, to every human creature, for
God's sake; whether it be to the king, as excelling;
14 Or to governors, as sent by him for the punishment
15 of evil doers, and for the praise of the good: For
so is the will of God, that by doing well, you may
16 silence the ignorance of foolish men: As free, and
not as making liberty a cloke of malice, but as the
17 servants of God. Honour all men: Love the broth-
18 erhood: fear God: honour the king: Servants, be
subject to your masters with all fear; not only to the
19 good, and gentle, but also to the froward. For this
is thankworthy, if for conscience towards God, a man
20 endure sorrows, suffering wrongfully. For what
glory is it, if, sinning and being buffeted, you suffer
it? But if, doing well, you suffer patiently, this is
21 thankworthy before God. For unto this you have been
called: because Christ also suffered for us, leaving you
22 an example, that you should follow his steps; Who
did no sin, neither was guile found in his mouth;
23 Who, when he was reviled, did not revile: when he
suffered, he threatened not; but delivered himself to
24 him that judged him unjustly: Who his own self bore
our sins in his body upon the tree; that we, being
dead to sins, should live to justice: by whose stripes
25 you were healed. For you were as sheep going
astray: but you are now converted to the pastor and
bishop of your souls.

CHAP. III. v. 1. In like manner also let wives be subject to
their husbands; that if any believe not the
word, they may be gained without the word, by the
2 conversation of the wives, Considering your chaste
3 conversation with fear. Whose adorning let it not
be the outward plaiting of the hair, or the wearing
4 of gold, or the putting on of apparel; But the hidden man of the heart in the incorruptibility of a
quiet and a meek spirit, which is rich in the sight of
5 God. For after this manner heretofore also the
holy women, hoping in God, adorned themselves,

6 being subject to their own husbands: As Sara
obeyed Abraham, calling him lord; whose daughters
you are, doing well, and not fearing any trouble.
7 Ye husbands, likewise, dwelling with them according
to knowledge, giving honour to the woman as to
the weaker vessel, and as to the co-heirs of the grace
8 of life; that your prayers be not hindered. And
finally, be ye all of one mind, having compassion
one of another, loving brotherhood, merciful, modest,
9 humble: Not rendering evil for evil, nor railing for
railing, but on the contrary, blessing: for unto this
are you called, that by inheritance you may possess
10 a blessing. For he that will love life, and see good
days, let him refrain his tongue from evil, and his
11 lips that they speak no guile. Let him decline from
evil, and do good: let him seek peace, and pursue it:
12 Because the eyes of the Lord are upon the just, and
his ears unto their prayers: but the countenance of
13 the Lord against them that do evil things. And
who is he that can hurt you, if you be zealous of
14 good? But if also you suffer anything for justice
sake, blessed are ye. And be not afraid of their
15 terror, and be not troubled. But sanctify the Lord
Christ in your heart, being always ready to satisfy
every one that asketh you a reason of that hope
16 which is in you. But with modesty and fear, having
a good conscience; that whereas they speak evil of
you, they may be ashamed who falsely accuse your
17 good conversation in Christ. For it is better doing
well (if such be the will of God) to suffer, than
18 doing ill. Because Christ also died once for our sins,
the just for the unjust, that he might offer us to God,
being put to death, indeed, in the flesh, but brought
19 to life by the Spirit. In which also he came and
20 preached to those spirits who were in prison: Who
in time past had been incredulous, when they waited
for the patience of God in the days of Noe, when
the ark was a building: in which a few, that is, eight
21 souls, were saved by water. Whereunto baptism
being of the like form, now saveth you also; not the
putting away of the filth of the flesh, but the exami-
nation of a good conscience towards God by the

22 resurrection of Jesus Christ, Who is on the right
hand of God, swallowing up death, that we might
become heirs of life everlasting; he being gone into
heaven, the angels, and powers, and virtues, being
made subject to him.

CHAP. IV. } Christ, therefore, having suffered in the flesh,
v. 1. } be ye also armed with the same thought:
for he that hath suffered in the flesh, hath ceased
2 from sins: That now as to the rest of his time in
the flesh, he may live not according to the desires of
3 men, but according to the will of God. For the
time past is sufficient to have fulfilled the will of the
Gentiles, for them who have walked in riotousness,
lusts, excess of wine, revelings, banquetings, and
4 unlawful worshipping of idols. Wherein they think
it strange, that you run not with them into the same
5 confusion of riotousness, speaking evil of *you:* Who
shall render an account to him, who is ready to judge
6 the living and the dead. For this cause also was
the gospel preached to the dead; that they might be
judged indeed, according to men in the flesh, but
7 may live according to God in the Spirit. But the
end of all approacheth. Be prudent, therefore, and
8 watch in prayers. But before all things have a
mutual charity among yourselves: for charity cover-
9 eth a multitude of sins. Using hospitality towards
10 one another without murmuring. As every man
hath received grace, ministering the same one to
another, as good stewards of the manifold grace of
11 God. If any speak, *let him speak* as the words of
God: if any man minister, *let it be* as from the
power which God administereth; that in all things
God may be honoured through Jesus Christ: to
whom is glory and dominion for ever and ever.
12 Amen. Most dearest, think not strange the burning
heat which is to try you, as if some new thing hap-
13 pened to you: But rejoice, being partakers of the
sufferings of Christ; that when his glory shall be
revealed, you may also be glad with exceeding joy.
14 If you be reproached for the name of Christ, you
shall be happy: for that which is of the honour,

glory, and power of God, and that which is his
15 Spirit, resteth upon you. But let none of you suffer
as a murderer, or a thief, or a railer, or as coveting
16 the goods of others: But if as a Christian, let him
not be ashamed: but let him glorify God in that
17 name. For the time is that judgment should begin
at the house of God. And if first at us, what shall
be the end of those who believe not the gospel of
18 God? And if the just man shall scarcely be saved,
where shall the wicked and the sinner appear?
19 Therefore also they, who suffer according to the will
of God, let them commend their souls in good deeds
to the faithful Creator.

CHAP. V. v. 1. } The ancients, therefore, that are among you, I
beseech, who am myself also an ancient and
a witness of Christ, as also a partaker of that glory
2 which is to be revealed in time to come: Feed the
flock of God which is among you; taking care
thereof not by constraint, but willingly according to
God: neither for the sake of filthy lucre, but volunta-
3 rily: Neither as domineering over the Clergy, but
being made a pattern of the flock from the heart.
4 And when the prince of pastors shall appear, you
5 shall receive a never-fading crown of glory. In like
manner, ye young men, be subject to the ancients.
And do ye all insinuate humility one to another: for
God resisteth the proud, and giveth grace to the
6 humble. Be you humbled, therefore, under the mighty
hand of God; that he may exalt you in the time of
7 visitation: Casting all your solicitude upon him;
8 for he hath care of you. Be sober and watch: because your adversary the devil, as a roaring lion,
9 goeth about seeking whom he may devour: Whom
resist ye, strong in faith; knowing that the same
affliction befalleth your brethren who are in the world.
10 But the God of all grace, who hath called us unto
his eternal glory in Christ Jesus, when you have
suffered a little, will himself perfect, and confirm,
11 and establish you. To him be glory and dominion
12 for ever and ever. Amen. By Silvanus, a faithful
brother unto you, as I think, I have written briefly;

beseeching and testifying, that this is the true grace
13 of God, wherein you stand. The church which is in
Babylon, elected together, saluteth you: and *so doth*
14 my son Mark. Salute one another with a holy kiss.
Grace unto you all, who are in Christ Jesus. Amen.

THE SECOND EPISTLE OF ST. PETER THE APOSTLE.

CHAP. I. v. 1. Simon Peter, a servant and an apostle of Jesus
Christ, to them who have obtained equal faith
with us, in the justice of our God and Saviour Jesus
2 Christ. Grace to you and peace be fulfilled in the
knowledge of God, and of Christ Jesus our Lord:
3 According as all things of his divine power, which
appertain to life and piety, are given to us, through
the knowledge of him who hath called us by his own
4 proper glory and virtue, By whom he hath given
us very great and precious promises; that by these
you may be made partakers of the divine nature;
flying from the corruption of that concupiscence
5 which is in the world. And you, giving all diligence,
join with your faith, virtue; and with virtue, knowl-
6 edge: And with knowledge, abstinence; and with
7 abstinence, patience; and with patience, piety; And
with piety, brotherly love; and with brotherly love,
8 charity. For if these things be with you, and abound,
they will make you to be neither empty, nor unfruit-
9 ful in the knowledge of our Lord Jesus Christ. For
he that hath not these things with him, is blind, and
groping, forgetting his being purged from his old sins.
10 Wherefore, brethren, labour the more, that by good
works you may make sure your vocation and election:
for doing these things, you shall not sin at any time.
11 For so an entrance shall be ministered to you abundantly into the everlasting kingdom of our Lord and
12 Saviour Jesus Christ. For which cause I will begin
to admonish you always of these things; though, indeed, you know them and are confirmed in the
13 present truth. But I think it just, as long as I am
in this tabernacle, to stir you up by admonition:
14 Being assured that the putting off of *this* my taber-

nacle is at hand, even according as our Lord Jesus
15 Christ hath signified to me. And I will endeavor,
that you frequently have after my decease, whereby
16 you may keep a memory of these things. For we
have not, by following artificial fables, made known
to you the power and presence of our Lord Jesus
Christ; but we were eye-witnesses of his greatness.
17 For he received from God the Father honour and
glory; this voice coming down to him from the excellent glory: This is my beloved Son, in whom I am
18 well pleased; hear ye him. And this voice we
heard brought from heaven, when we were with
19 him in the holy mount. And we have the word of
prophecy more firm: to which you do well to attend,
as to a light shining in a dark place until the day
dawn, and the morning-star rise in your hearts:
20 Understanding this first, that no prophecy of the
21 Scripture is made by private interpretation. For
prophecy came not by the will of man at any time;
but the holy men of God spoke, inspired by the Holy
Ghost.

CHAP. II. v. 1. But there were also false prophets among the
people; even as there shall be lying teachers
among you, who shall bring in sects of perdition, and
deny the Lord who bought them, bringing upon
2 themselves swift destruction. And many shall follow their luxuries, by whom the way of truth shall
3 be blasphemed: And through covetousness with
feigned words they shall make merchandise of you;
whose judgment now of a long time ceaseth not, and
4 their destruction slumbereth not. For if God spared
not the angels that sinned, but having cast them down
into the place of torments delivered them into the
chains of hell to be tormented, to be reserved unto
5 judgment; And spared not the original world, but
preserved Noe the eighth person, a preacher of
justice, bringing in the deluge upon the world of the
6 impious. And reducing the cities of the Sodomites,
and of the Gomorrhites into ashes, condemned them
to destruction; making them an example to those
7 that should after act wickedly: And delivered Lot, a

just man oppressed by the injustice and lewd conver-
8 sation of the wicked: For in sight and hearing he
was just; dwelling among them, who from day to
day vexed the just soul with *their* impious deeds:
9 The Lord knoweth how to deliver the godly out of
temptation; but to reserve the unjust unto the day
10 of judgment to be tormented: And especially those
who walk after the flesh in the lust of uncleanness,
and despise governments, audacious, pleasing themselves, they fear not to bring in sects, blaspheming:
11 Whereas angels, though they are greater in strength
and power, bear not an execrable judgment against
12 themselves. But these men, as irrational beasts,
naturally tending to the snare, and to destruction,
blaspheming those things which they know not, shall
13 perish in their corruption, Receiving the reward of
injustice, counting pleasure the delights of a day;
stains and blemishes, flowing in delicacies, rioting in
14 their feasts with you, Having eyes full of adultery,
and of never ceasing sin: alluring unstable souls,
having their heart exercised with covetousness, sons
15 of malediction: Forsaking the right way, they have
gone astray, having followed the way of Balaam of
16 Bosor, who loved the wages of iniquity: But had a
check of his madness: a dumb beast, subject to the
yoke, speaking with man's voice, forbade the folly of
17 the prophet. These are fountains without water, and
clouds tossed with whirlwinds, to whom the mist of
18 darkness is reserved. For, speaking swelling words
of vanity, they allure in desires of the flesh of
riotousness those, who had escaped a little from them
19 who converse in error: Promising them liberty,
when they themselves are slaves of corruption: for
by whom a man is overcome, of the same also he is
20 the slave. For if having fled from the pollutions of
the world through the knowledge of our Lord and
Saviour Jesus Christ, being again entangled in them,
they are overcome: their latter state is become unto
21 them worse than the former. For it had been better
for them not to have known the way of justice, than,
after they have known it, to turn back from that holy
22 commandment, which was delivered to them. For

that of the true proverb hath happened to them:
The dog is returned to his own vomit: and the sow
that was washed, to her wallowing in the mire.

CHAP. III. } Behold, this is the second epistle I write to
v. 1. } you, my dearly beloved, in which I stir up
2 by admonition your sincere mind: That you may
be mindful of those words which I told you before
from the holy prophets, and of your apostles, of the
3 precepts of the Lord and Saviour. Knowing this
first, that in the last days there shall come scoffers
with deceit, walking according to their own lusts,
4 Saying: Where is his promise, or his coming? For
since the fathers slept, all things continue so from the
5 beginning of the creation, For this they are wilfully
ignorant of, that the heavens were before, and the
earth, out of water, and through water, consisting by
6 the word of God: Whereby the world that then
7 was, being overflowed with water, perished. But
the heavens which now are, and the earth, by the
same word are kept in store, reserved unto fire
against the day of judgment, and perdition of wicked
8 men. But be not ignorant, my beloved, of this one
thing, that one day with the Lord is as a thousand
9 years, and a thousand years as one day. The Lord
delayeth not his promise, as some imagine; but
beareth patiently for your sake, not willing that any
should perish, but that all should return to penance.
10 But the day of the Lord shall come as a thief, in
which the heavens shall pass away with great violence;
and the elements shall be dissolved with heat; and
the earth and the works that are in it, shall be burnt
11 up. Seeing, then, that all these things are to be
dissolved, what manner of people ought you to be in
12 holy conversation and godliness, Waiting for, and
hastening unto the coming of the day of the Lord,
by which the heavens being on fire shall be dissolved,
and the elements shall melt with the burning heat of
13 fire? But we look for new heavens and a new earth,
according to his promise, in which justice dwelleth.
14 Wherefore, dearly beloved, waiting for these things,
be diligent that you may be found before him unspot-

15 ted and blameless in peace: And account the long-
bearing of our Lord, salvation: as also our most
dear brother Paul, according to the wisdom given to
16 him, hath written to you, As also in all *his* epistles,
speaking in them of these things: in which are some
things hard to be understood, which the unlearned
and unstable wrest, as also the other Scriptures, to
17 their own perdition. You, therefore, brethren, knowing these things before, beware; lest, being led away
by the error of the unwise, you fall from your own
18 steadfastness. But increase in grace, and in the
knowledge of our Lord and Saviour Jesus Christ.
To him be glory both now and unto the day of
eternity. Amen.

THE CATHOLIC EPISTLE OF ST. JAMES THE APOSTLE.

CHAP. I. v. 1. James, a servant of God, and of our Lord
Jesus Christ, to the twelve tribes which are
2 dispersed, greeting. My brethren, count it all joy,
3 when you shall fall into divers temptations; Knowing that the trying of your faith worketh patience.
4 And patience hath a perfect work; that you may be
5 perfect and entire, deficient in nothing. But if any
of you want wisdom, let him ask of God, who giveth
to all abundantly, and upbraideth not: and it shall
6 be given him. But let him ask in faith, nothing
wavering: for he that wavereth is like a wave of
the sea, that is moved and carried about by the wind.
7 Therefore, let not that man think that he shall receive
8 any thing of the Lord. A double-minded man is
9 inconstant in all his ways. But let the brother of
10 low condition glory in his exaltation: But the rich,
in his being low, because as the flower of the grass,
11 he shall pass away: For the sun rose with a burning
heat, and parched the grass; and the flower thereof
fell off; and the beauty of the shape thereof perished:
so also shall the rich man fade away in his ways.
12 Blessed is the man that endureth temptation: for
when he hath been proved, he shall receive the
crown of life, which God hath promised to them

13 that love him. Let no man, when he is tempted, say
that he is tempted of God: for God is not a tempter
14 of evils: and he tempteth no man. But every man
is tempted, being drawn away by his own concupi-
15 scence, and allured. Then when concupiscence hath
conceived, it bringeth forth sin: but sin, when it is
16 completed, begetteth death. Do not err, therefore,
17 my dearest brethren. Every best gift, and every
perfect gift, is from above, coming down from the
Father of lights, with whom there is no change, nor
18 shadow of vicissitude. For of his own will hath
he begotten us by the word of truth, that we might
19 be some beginning of his creatures. You know, my
dearest brethren: and let every man be swift to hear;
20 but slow to speak, and slow to anger. For the anger
21 of man worketh not the justice of God. Wherefore,
casting away all uncleanness, and abundance of malice,
with meekness receive the ungrafted word, which is
22 able to save your souls. But be ye doers of the
word, and not hearers only, deceiving your own
23 selves. For if a man be a hearer of the word, and
not a doer; he shall be compared to a man beholding
24 his natural countenance in a glass: For he beheld
himself, and went his way, and presently forgot what
25 manner of man he was. But he that hath looked
into the perfect law of liberty, and hath continued in
it, not becoming a forgetful hearer, but a doer of the
26 work; this man shall be blessed in his deed. And
if any man think himself to be religious, not bridling
his tongue, but deceiving his own heart, this man's
27 religion is vain. Religion pure and unspotted with
God and the Father is this: To visit the fatherless
and widows in their tribulation, and to keep one's
self undefiled from this world.

CHAP. II. v. 1. } My brethren, have not the faith of our Lord
Jesus Christ of glory with respect of persons.
2 For if there come into your assembly a man having
a gold ring in fine apparel, and there come in also a
3 poor man in mean attire, And you cast your eyes
on him that is clothed with the fine apparel, and say
to him: Sit thou here in a good place: and say to

the poor man: Stand thou there, or sit under my
4 foot-stool: Do you not judge within yourselves, and
5 are become judges of unjust thoughts? Hearken, my
dearest brethren: hath not God chosen the poor of
this world, rich in faith, and heirs of the kingdom
which God hath promised to them that love him?
6 But you have dishonored the poor. Do not the
rich oppress you by might; and do not they draw
7 you before the judgment seats? Do not they blaspheme the good name that is invoked upon you?
8 If then you fulfil the royal law, according to the
Scriptures: Thou shalt love thy neighbour as thy-
9 self; you do well. But if you have respect to persons, you commit sin, being reproved by the law as
10 transgressors. Now whosoever shall keep the whole
law, but offend in one *point*, is become guilty of all.
11 For he that said, Thou shalt not commit adultery,
said also, Thou shalt not kill. Now if thou do not
commit adultery, but shall kill, thou art become a
12 transgressor of the law. So speak ye, and so do,
13 as being to be judged by the law of liberty. For
judgment without mercy, to him that hath not done
mercy: and mercy exalteth *itself* above judgment.
14 What shall it profit, my brethren, if a man say he
hath faith, but hath not works? Shall faith be able
15 to save him? And if a brother or sister be naked,
16 and want daily food, And one of you say to them:
Go in peace, be you warmed and filled; yet give
them not those things that are necessary for the body,
17 what shall it profit? Even so faith, if it have not
18 works, is dead in itself. But some man will say:
Thou hast faith; and I have works: Show me thy
faith without works; and I will show thee my faith,
19 by works. Thou believest that there is one God.
Thou doest well: the devils also believe and trem-
20 ble. But wilt thou know, O vain man, that faith
21 without works is dead? Was not Abraham our father justified by works, offering up Isaac his son
22 upon the altar? Seest thou that faith did co-operate
with his works; and by works faith was made per-
23 fect? And the Scripture was fulfilled, saying:
Abraham believed God; and it was reputed to him

to justice: and he was called the friend of God.
24 Do you see that by works a man is justified, and not
25 by faith only? And in like manner also Rabah
the harlot, was not she justified by works, receiving the messengers, and sending them out another
26 way? For as the body without the spirit is dead,
so also faith without works is dead.

CHAP. III. } Be not many masters, my brethren, knowing
v. 1–2. } that you receive the greater judgment. For
in many things we all offend. If any man offend
not in word, the same is a perfect man. He is able
also with a bridle to turn about the whole body.
3 For if we put bits into the mouths of horses that
they may obey us, and we turn about their whole
4 body. Behold also ships, whereas they are great,
and are driven by strong winds, yet are they turned
about with a small helm, whithersoever the force of
5 the governor willeth. Even so the tongue is, indeed,
a little member, and boasteth great things. Behold
6 how small a fire kindleth a great wood. And the
tongue is a fire, a world of iniquity. The tongue is
placed among our members, which defileth the whole
body, and setteth on fire the wheel of our nativity,
7 being set on fire by hell. For every kind of beasts,
and of birds, and of serpents, and of the rest, is
8 tamed, and hath been tamed by mankind: But
the tongue no man can tame; a restless evil, full of
9 deadly poison. By it we bless God and the Father:
and by it we curse men, who are made after the
10 likeness of God. Out of the same mouth proceedeth
blessing and cursing. My brethren, these things
11 ought not so to be. Doth a fountain send forth
through the same passage sweet and bitter water?
12 Can the fig-tree, my brethren, bear grapes, or the
vine, figs? So neither can the salt water yield sweet.
13 Who is a wise man, and endued with knowledge
among you? Let him show, by a good conversation,
14 his work in the meekness of wisdom. But if you
have bitter zeal, and there be contentions in your
hearts; glory not, and be not liars against the truth.
15 For this is not wisdom, descending from above; but

16 earthly, sensual, diabolical. For where envying and
contention is, there is inconstancy and every evil
17 work. But the wisdom which is from above, first
indeed is chaste, then peaceable, modest, easy to be
persuaded, consenting to the good, full of mercy,
and good fruits, without judging, without dissimula-
18 tion. And the fruit of justice is sown in peace, to
them that make peace.

CHAP. IV. v. 1. From whence are wars and contentions among
you? Come they not hence? from your
2 concupiscences, which war in your members? You
covet, and have not: you kill, and envy, and cannot
obtain: you contend, and war: and you have not,
3 because you ask not. You ask, and receive not;
because you ask amiss; that you may consume it on
4 your concupiscences. Adulterers, know you not that
the friendship of this world, is the enemy of God?
Whosoever, therefore, will be a friend of this world,
5 becometh an enemy of God. Or do you think that
the scripture saith in vain: To envy doth the spirit
6 covet, which dwelleth in you? But he giveth greater
grace. Wherefore he saith: God resisteth the proud,
7 and giveth grace to the humble. Be subject, therefore, to God: but resist the devil, and he will fly
8 from you. Approach to God, and he will approach
to you. Cleanse your hands, ye sinners: and purify
9 your hearts, ye double-minded. Be afflicted, and
mourn, and weep: let your laughter be turned into
10 mourning, and your joy into sorrow. Be humble
in the sight of the Lord; and he will exalt you.
11 Detract not one another, brethren. He that detracteth
his brother, or he that judgeth his brother, detracteth
the law, and judgeth the law. But if thou judge
the law, thou art not a doer of the law, but a judge.
12 There is one lawgiver, and judge, who is able to
13 destroy and to deliver. But who art thou, who
judgest thy neighbour? Behold now, you who say:
To-day or to-morrow we will go into such a city;
and there we will spend a year, and will traffic, and
14 make gain: Whereas you know not what shall be on
15 the morrow. For what is your life? It is a vapour

which appeareth for a little while, and afterwards
shall vanish away. For that you should say: If
the Lord will; and, If we shall live, we will do this
16 or that. But now you glory in your arrogancies. All
17 such glorying is wicked. To him, therefore, who
knoweth to do good, and doeth it not, to him it is sin.

CHAP. V. v. 1–2. Go to, now, ye rich men; weep and howl for
your miseries that shall come upon you. Your
riches are putrified, and your garments are moth-
3 eaten. Your gold and silver is rusted: and the
rust of them shall be for a testimony against you;
and shall eat your flesh as fire. You have stored
4 up to yourselves wrath against the last days. Behold, the hire of the labourers, who have reaped
your fields of which you have defrauded them, crieth
out; and the cry of them hath entered into the ears
5 of the Lord of Sabaoth. You have feasted upon
earth; and in luxuries you have nourished your
6 hearts in the day of slaughter. You have condemned
and put to death the just one; and he resisteth you
7 not. Be patient, therefore, brethren, until the coming of the Lord. Behold, the husbandman waiteth
for the precious fruit of the earth, patiently bearing
8 till he receive the early and the latter rain. Be you,
therefore, also patient, and strengthen your hearts:
9 for the coming of the Lord draweth near. Grudge
not, brethren, one against another, that you may not
be judged. Behold, the Judge standeth before the
10 door. Take, my brethren, for an example of suffering evil, of labour and patience, the prophets, who
11 spoke in the name of the Lord. Behold, we account
them blessed, who have suffered. You have heard
of the patience of Job: and you have seen the end
of the Lord, that the Lord is merciful and compas-
12 sionate. But above all things, my brethren, swear
not, neither by heaven, nor by the earth, nor by any
other oath. But let your speech be: Yea, yea: no,
13 no: that you fall not under judgment. Is any of
you sad? Let him pray. Is he cheerful in mind?
14 Let him sing psalms. Is any man sick among you?
Let him bring in the priests of the church, and let

them pray over him, anointing him with oil, in the
15 name of the Lord: And the prayer of faith shall
save the sick man: and the Lord shall raise him up:
and if he be in sins, they shall be forgiven him.
16 Confess, therefore, your sins one to another; and
pray for one another, that you may be saved: for
the continual prayer of a just man availeth much.
17 Elias was a man passible like unto us: and with
prayer he prayed that it might not rain upon the
earth; and it rained not for three years and six
18 months. And he prayed again: and the heaven gave
19 rain, and the earth yielded her fruit. My brethren,
if any of you shall err from the truth, and any one
20 convert him: He must know, that he who causeth a
sinner to be converted from the error of his way,
shall save his soul from death, and shall cover a
multitude of sins.

THE FIRST EPISTLE OF ST. JOHN THE APOSTLE.

CHAP. I. v. 1. That which was from the beginning, which we
have heard, which we have seen with our eyes,
which we have diligently looked upon, and our hands
2 have handled, concerning the word of life: For the
life was manifested: and we have seen, and do bear
witness, and declare unto you the eternal life, which
3 was with the Father, and hath appeared to us: That
which we have seen and have heard, we declare unto
you; that you also may have fellowship with us, and our
fellowship may be with the Father, and with his Son
4 Jesus Christ. And these things we write to you, that
5 you may rejoice, and your joy may be full. And this
is the declaration which we have heard from him, and
declare unto you: That God is light; and that in him
6 there is no darkness. If we say that we have fellowship with him, and walk in darkness, we lie, and do
7 not the truth. But if we walk in the light, as he also
is in the light; we have fellowship one towards another, and the blood of Jesus Christ his Son cleanseth
8 us from all sin. If we say that we have no sin, we
9 deceive ourselves, and the truth is not in us. If we

confess our sins, he is faithful and just, to forgive us
10 our sins, and to cleanse us from all iniquity. If we
say that we have not sinned, we make him a liar; and
his word is not in us.

CHAP. II. } My little children, these things I write to you,
v. 1. } that you may not sin. But if any man sin,
we have an advocate with the Father, Jesus Christ
2 the just: And he is the propitiation for our sins; and
not for ours only, but also for those of the whole
3 world. And in this we do know that we have known
4 him, if we keep his commandments. He that saith
he knoweth him, and keepeth not his commandments,
5 is a liar; and the truth is not in him. But whosoever keepeth his word, the charity of God is truly
perfect in him: and by this we know that we are in
6 him. He that saith he abideth in him, ought himself
7 also to walk, even as he walked. My dearest, I write
not a new commandment to you, but an old commandment, which you had from the beginning: The old
commandment is the word which you have heard.
8 Again a new commandment I write to you, which
thing is true both in him and in you: because the
9 darkness is past, and the true light now shineth. He
that saith he is in the light, and hateth his brother, is
10 in darkness even until now. He that loveth his brother abideth in the light, and there is no scandal in
11 him. But he that hateth his brother is in darkness,
and walketh in darkness, and knoweth not whither he
goeth: because the darkness hath blinded his eyes.
12 I write to you, little children, because your sins are
13 forgiven you for his name's sake. I write to you,
fathers, because you have known him, who is from the
beginning. I write to you, young men, because you
14 have overcome the wicked one. I write to you, infants,
because you have known the Father. I write to you,
young men, because you are strong, and the word of
God abideth in you, and you have overcome the
15 wicked one. Love not the world, nor those things
which are in the world. If any man love the world,
16 the charity of the Father is not in him: For all that
is in the world, is the concupiscence of the flesh, and

the concupiscence of the eyes, and the pride of life:
17 which is not of the Father, but is of the world. And
the world passeth away, and the concupiscence thereof.
But he that doeth the will of God, abideth for ever.
18 Little children, it is the last hour: and as you have
heard that Antichrist cometh, even now there are
many Antichrists: whereby we know that it is the last
19 hour. They went out from us: but they were not of
us. For if they had been of us, they would no doubt
have continued with us: but that they might be made
20 manifest, that they are not all of us. But you have
an unction from the Holy One; and you know all
21 things. I have not written to you as to such as know
not the truth, but as to such as know it; and that no
22 lie is from the truth. Who is a liar, but he who denieth that Jesus is the Christ? He is Antichrist, who
23 denieth the Father and the Son. Whosoever denieth
the Son, neither hath he the Father. He that con-
24 fesseth the Son, hath the Father also. Let that which
you have heard from the beginning, abide in you: If
what you have heard from the beginning shall abide
in you, you also shall abide in the Son, and in the
25 Father. And this is the promise which he hath prom-
26 ised to us, eternal life. These things have I written
27 to you concerning them that seduce you. And the
unction, which you have received from him, let it
abide in you. And you have no need that any one
should teach you; but as his unction teacheth you
concerning all things, and it is truth, and is not a lie.
28 And as it hath taught you, abide in him. And now,
little children, abide in him; that when he shall appear, we may have confidence, and not be confounded
29 by him at his coming, If you know that he is just,
know also that every one who doeth justice, is born of
him.

CHAP. III. v. 1. } Behold what manner of charity the Father
hath bestowed upon us, that we should be
named, and should be the sons of God. Therefore,
the world hath not known us: because it hath not
2 known him. Dearly beloved, we are now the sons of
God: and it hath not yet appeared what we shall

be. We know, that when he shall appear, we shall be
3 like to him: because we shall see him as he is. And
every man that hath this hope in him, sanctifieth him-
4 self, as he also is holy. Whosoever committeth sin,
5 committeth also iniquity: and sin is iniquity. And
you know that he appeared to take away our sins:
6 and in him there is no sin. Whosoever abideth in
him, sinneth not: and whosoever sinneth, hath not seen
7 him, nor known him. Little children, let no one deceive you. He that doeth justice, is just; as he also
8 is just. He that committeth sin is of the devil: for
the devil sinneth from the beginning. For this pur-
pose the Son of God appeared, that he might destroy
9 the works of the devil. Every one that is born of
God, doth not commit sin: for his seed remaineth in
him; and he cannot sin, because he is born of God.
10 In this the children of God are manifest, and the children of the devil. Whosoever is not just, is not of
11 God, nor is he that loveth not his brother: For this
is the declaration which you have heard from the be-
12 ginning, that you should love one another. Not as
Cain, who was of the wicked one, and killed his brother. And for what cause did he kill him? Because
13 his own works were evil, and his brother's just. Won-
14 der not, brethren, if the world hate you. We know
that we have passed from death to life; because we
love the brethren. He that loveth not, abideth in
15 death: Whosoever hateth his brother, is a murderer.
And you know that no murderer hath eternal life
16 abiding in himself. In this we have known the charity
of God, because he hath laid down his life for us: and
17 we ought to lay down our lives for the brethren. He
that hath the substance of this world, and shall see
his brother in need, and shall shut up his bowels from
18 him; how doth the charity of God abide in him? My
little children, let us not love in word, nor in tongue,
19 but in deed, and in truth. In this we know that we
are of the truth: and in his sight we shall persuade
20 our hearts. For if our heart reprehend us, God is
21 greater than our heart, and knoweth all things. Dearly
beloved, if our heart do not reprehend us, we have
22 confidence towards God: And whatsoever we shall

ask, we shall receive of him: because we keep his
commandments, and do those things that are pleas-
23 ing in his sight. And this is his commandment: that
we should believe in the name of his Son Jesus Christ;
and love one another, as he hath given commandment
24 unto us. And he that keepeth his commandments,
abideth in him, and he in him: and in this we know
that he abideth in us, from the Spirit which he hath
given us.

CHAP. IV. v. 1. Dearly beloved, believe not every spirit; but
try the spirits, whether they be of God: be-
cause many false prophets are gone out into the world.
2 By this is the Spirit of God known: every spirit, that
confesseth Jesus Christ to have come in the flesh, is of
3 God: And every spirit that dissolveth Jesus, is not
of God: and this is Antichrist, of whom you have
heard that he cometh, and he is now already in the
4 world. You are of God, little children, and have overcome him; because greater is he that is in you, than
5 he that is in the world. They are of the world: therefore of the world they speak, and the world heareth
6 them. We are of God. He that knoweth God, heareth us: He that is not of God, heareth us not: by
this we know the Spirit of truth, and the spirit of
7 error. Dearly beloved, let us love one another: for
charity is of God. And every one that loveth, is born
8 of God, and knoweth God. He that loveth not, know-
9 eth not God: for God is charity. By this hath appeared the charity of God in us; because God hath
sent his only begotten Son into the world, that we
10 might live through him. In this is charity: not as if
we have loved God, but because he first loved us, and
11 sent his Son a propitiation for our sins. My dearest,
if God hath so loved us, we ought also to love one an-
12 other. No man hath seen God at any time. If we
love one another, God abideth in us, and his charity is
13 perfected in us. By this we know that we abide in
him, and he in us; because he hath given us of his
14 Spirit: And we have seen, and do testify, that the
Father hath sent his Son the Saviour of the world.
15 Whosoever shall confess that Jesus is the Son of God,

16 God abideth in him, and he in God. And we have
known, and have believed the charity, which God hath
to us. God is charity: and he that abideth in charity,
17 abideth in God, and God in him. In this is the charity
of God perfected with us, that we may have confidence in the day of judgment: because as he is, we
18 also are in this world. Fear is not in charity: but
perfect charity casteth out fear; because fear hath
pain: and he that feareth, is not perfect in charity.
19 Let us, therefore, love God, because God first hath
20 loved us. If any man say, I love God, and hateth
his brother, he is a liar. For he that loveth not his
brother, whom he seeth, how can he love God, whom
21 he seeth not? And this commandment we have from
God, that he, who loveth God, love also his brother.

CHAP. V. v. 1. } Whosoever believeth that Jesus is the Christ,
is born of God. And every one that loveth
him that begot, loveth him also who was born of him.
2 *In this we know that we love the children of* God,
3 when we love God, and keep his commandments. For
this is the charity of God, that we keep his command-
4 ments: and his commandments are not heavy. For
whatsoever is born of God, overcometh the world:
and this is the victory which overcometh the world,
5 our faith. Who is he that overcometh the world, but
6 he that believeth that Jesus is the Son of God? This
is he that came by water and blood, Jesus Christ; not
in water only, but in water and blood. And it is the
7 Spirit that testifieth, that Christ is the truth. For
there are three that give testimony in heaven; the
Father, the Word, and the Holy Ghost: and these
8 three are one. And there are three that give testimony on earth; the spirit, the water, and the blood:
9 and these three are one. If we receive the testimony
of men, the testimony of God is greater: for this is
the testimony of God, which is greater, because he
10 hath testified of his Son. He that believeth in the Son
of God, hath the testimony of God in himself. He
that believeth not the Son, maketh him a liar; because he believeth not in the testimony which God
11 hath testified of his Son. And this is the testimony,

that God hath given to us eternal life: and this life
12 is in his Son. He that hath the Son, hath life: he
13 that hath not the Son, hath not life. These things I
write to you, that you may know that you have eternal
14 life; who believe in the name of the Son of God. And
this is the confidence which we have in him: that
whatsoever we shall ask, according to his will, he hear-
15 eth us. And we know that he heareth us whatsoever
we ask: we know that we have the petitions which
16 we request of him. He that knoweth his brother to
sin a sin *which* is not unto death, let him ask, and life
shall be given to him, that sinneth not to death. There
is a sin unto death: I do not say that any one should
17 ask for it. All iniquity is sin: and there is a sin unto
18 death. We know that every one, who is born of God,
sinneth not: but the generation of God preserveth
19 him, and the wicked one toucheth him not. We know
that we are of God: and the whole world is seated in
20 wickedness. And we know that the Son of God is
come, and hath given us understanding, that we may
know the true God, and may be in his true Son.
21 This is the true God, and eternal life. Little children,
keep yourselves from idols. Amen.

THE SECOND EPISTLE OF ST. JOHN THE APOSTLE.

CHAP. I. v. 1. } The ancient to the lady Elect and her children,
whom I love in truth, and not I only, but also
2 all they who have known the truth, For the sake of
the truth: which abideth in us, and shall be with us
3 for ever. Grace be with you, mercy, and peace from
God the Father, and from Christ Jesus the Son of the
4 Father, in truth, and charity. I was exceeding glad,
that I found of thy children walking in truth, as we
5 have received a commandment from the Father. And
now I beseech thee, lady, not as writing a new commandment to thee, but that which we have had from
6 the beginning, that we love one another. And this is
charity, that we walk according to his commandments.
For this is the commandment, that as you have heard
7 from the beginning, you should walk in it: For many
seducers are gone out into the world, who confess not

that Jesus Christ is come in the flesh: this is a seducer
8 and an antichrist. Look to yourselves, that you lose
not the things which you have wrought; but that you
9 may receive a full reward. Whosoever recedeth, and
continueth not in the doctrine of Christ, hath not God:
he that continueth in the doctrine, he hath both the
10 Father and the Son. If any man come to you, and
bring not this doctrine, receive him not into the house,
11 nor say to him, God save you. For he that saith to
him: God save you, communicateth with his wicked
12 works. Having more things to write unto you, I
would not by paper and ink: for I hope that I shall
be with you, and speak face to face; that your joy
13 may be full. The children of thy sister Elect salute
thee.

THE THIRD EPISTLE OF ST. JOHN THE APOSTLE.

CHAP. I. v. 1–2. } The ancient to the dearly beloved Gaius, whom
I love in truth. Dearly beloved, I make my
prayer that thou mayest prosper as to all things, and
be in health, even as thy soul doeth prosperously.
3 I was exceeding glad when the brethren came, and
gave testimony to the truth in thee, even as thou walk-
4 est in truth. I have no greater grace than this, to
5 hear that my children walk in truth. Dearly beloved,
thou doest faithfully whatsoever thou doest for the
6 brethren, and that for strangers, Who have given testimony of thy charity in the sight of the church; whom,
thou shalt do well, to bring forward on their way in a
7 manner worthy of God. Because, for his name's sake
8 they went forth, taking nothing of the Gentiles. We,
therefore, ought to receive such; that we may be fel-
9 low-helpers of the truth. I had written perhaps to
the church: but Diotrephes, who loveth to have the
10 pre-eminence among them, doth not receive us. Wherefore, if I come, I will publish his works which he doeth,
prating against us with malicious words: and as if
these things were not enough for him, neither doth he
himself receive the brethren: and those that do receive them he forbiddeth, and casteth out of the church.
11 Dearly beloved, follow not that which is evil, but that

which is good. He that doeth good, is of God: he
12 that doeth evil, hath not seen God. To Demetrius
testimony is given by all, and by the truth itself; yea,
and we also give testimony: and thou knowest that
13 our testimony is true. I had many things to write
unto thee: but I would not by ink and pen write to
14 thee. But I hope speedily to see thee; and we will
speak face to face. Peace be to thee. Our friends
salute thee. Salute the friends by name.

THE APOCALYPSE OF ST. JOHN THE APOSTLE.

CHAP. I. v. 1. The revelation of Jesus Christ, which God gave
to him to make known to his servants the things
which must shortly come to pass; and signified, send-
2 ing by his angel to his servant John, Who hath given
testimony to the word of God, and the testimony of
3 Jesus Christ, what things soever he hath seen. Blessed
is he, that readeth and heareth the words of this
prophecy; and keepeth those things which are written
4 in it: for the time is at hand. John to the seven
churches which are in Asia. Grace *be* unto you and
peace from him, who is, and who was, and who is to
come, and from the seven spirits which are before his
5 throne; And from Jesus Christ, who is the faithful
witness, the first begotten of the dead, and the prince
of the kings of the earth; who hath loved us, and
6 washed us from our sins in his own blood, And hath
made us a kingdom and priests to God and his Father; to him be glory and empire for ever and ever.
7 Amen. Behold, he cometh with the clouds: and every
eye shall see him, and they that pierced him. And
all the tribes of the earth shall bewail themselves be-
8 cause of him: Even so: Amen. I am Alpha, and
Omega, the beginning, and the end, saith the Lord
God, who is, and who was, and who is to come, the
9 Almighty. I John your brother, and sharer in tribulation, and in the kingdom, and patience in Christ
Jesus; was in the island, which is called Patmos, for
10 the word of God, and for the testimony of Jesus: I
was in spirit on the Lord's day, and heard behind
11 me a great voice, as of a trumpet, Saying: What thou

seest, write in a book ; and send to the seven churches
which are in Asia, to Ephesus, and to Smyrna, and to
Pergamus, and to Thyatira, and to Sardis, and to Phil-
12 adelphia, and to Laodicia. And I turned to see the
voice that spoke with me: and being turned, I saw
13 seven golden candlesticks. And in the midst of the
seven golden candlesticks, one like unto the Son of
man, clothed with a garment down to the feet, and
14 girded about near the paps with a golden girdle. And
his head, and hair, were white, like white wool, and
15 as snow, and his eyes were as a flame of fire, And
his feet like unto fine brass, as in a burning furnace,
16 and his voice as the sound of many waters: And he
had in his right hand seven stars: and from his mouth
came out a sharp two-edged sword: and his countenance shined as the sun shineth in its full strength.
17 And when I saw him, I fell at his feet as dead. And
he laid his right hand upon me, saying: Fear not: I
18 am the first and the last, And alive, and was dead;
and behold, I am living for ever and ever, and have
19 the keys of death and of hell. Write, therefore, the
things which thou hast seen, and which are, and which
20 must be done hereafter. The mystery of the seven
stars, which thou sawest in my right hand, and the
seven golden candlesticks: the seven stars are the
angels of the seven churches; and the seven candlesticks are the seven churches.

CHAP. II. v. 1. To the angel of the church of Ephesus write:
These things saith he, who holdeth the seven
stars in his right hand, who walketh in the midst of
2 the seven golden candlesticks: I know thy works, and
thy labour, and thy patience, and how thou canst not
bear evil men: and thou hast tried them, who say
they are apostles, and are not, and hast found them
3 liars: And thou hast patience, and hast borne for my
4 name, and hast not failed. But *this* I have against
5 thee, that thou hast left thy first charity. Be mindful,
therefore, from whence thou art fallen: and do penance,
and do the first works. Or else I come to thee, and
will remove thy candlestick out of its place, unless
6 thou shalt have done penance. But this thou hast,

that thou hatest the deeds of the Nicolaites, which I
7 also hate. He that hath an ear, let him hear what
the Spirit saith to the churches: To him, that overcometh, I will give to eat of the tree of life, which is
8 in the paradise of my God. And to the angel of the
church of Smyrna write: These things saith the First
9 and the Last; who was dead, and liveth: I know thy
tribulation and thy poverty; but thou art rich: and
thou art blasphemed by those who say they are Jews,
10 and are not, but are the synagogue of Satan. Fear
none of those things which thou shalt suffer. Behold,
the devil shall cast some of you into prison, that you
may be tried: and you shall have tribulation ten
days. Be thou faithful until death, and I will give
11 thee the crown of life. He that hath an ear, let him
hear what the Spirit saith to the churches: He that
shall overcome, shall not be hurt by the second death.
12 And to the angel of the church of Pergamus write:
These things saith he that hath the sharp two-edged
13 sword: I know where thou dwellest, where the seat
of Satan is: and thou holdest fast my name, and hast
not denied my faith. Even in those days Antipas *was*
my faithful witness, who was slain among you, where
14 Satan dwelleth. But I have a few things against thee:
because thou hast there them that hold the doctrine
of Balaam, who taught Balac to cast a stumbling-block
before the children of Israel, to eat and commit forni-
15 cation: So hast thou also them that hold the doctrine
16 of the Nicolaites. In like manner do penance: if not,
I will come to thee quickly; and will fight against
17 them with the sword of my mouth. He that hath an
ear, let him hear what the Spirit saith to the churches:
To him, that overcometh, I will give the hidden manna,
and will give him a white stone; and in the stone
a new name written, which no man knoweth, but he
18 that receiveth it. And to the angel of the church of
Thyatira write: These things saith the Son of God,
who hath eyes as a flame of fire, and his feet like
19 unto fine brass: I know thy works, and thy faith, and
thy charity, and ministry, and thy patience, and thy
20 last works which are more than the former. But I
have a few things against thee: because thou permit-

test the woman Jezabel, who calleth herself a prophet-
ess, to teach, and to seduce my servants, to commit
21 fornication, and to eat of things offered to idols. And
I gave her time to do penance: and she will not re-
22 pent of her fornication. Behold, I will cast her into
a bed: and they that commit adultery with her, shall
be in very great tribulation, unless they do penance
23 from their deeds. And I will kill her children with
death: and all the churches shall know, that I am he
who searcheth the reins and hearts: and I will give
to every one of you according to your works. But I
24 say to you, And to the rest who are at Thyatira:
Whosoever have not this doctrine, and who have not
known the depths of Satan, as they say, I will not put
25 upon you any other weight: Yet that which you have,
26 hold fast till I come. And he that shall overcome,
and keep my works unto the end, to him I will give
27 power over the nations; And he shall rule them with
a rod of iron; and as the vessel of a potter they shall
28 be broken; Even as I received from my Father: and I
29 will give him the morning star. He that hath an ear,
let him hear what the Spirit saith to the churches.

CHAP. III. v. 1. And to the angel of the church of Sardis
write: These things saith he, who hath the
seven Spirits of God, and the seven stars: I know thy
works, that thou hast the name of being alive, and
2 thou art dead. Be watchful, and strengthen the things
that remain, which are ready to die. For I find not
3 thy works full before my God. Have in mind, therefore, in what manner thou hast received and heard,
and observe, and do penance. If then thou shalt not
watch, I will come to thee as a thief; and thou shalt
4 not know at what hour I will come to thee. But thou
hast a few names in Sardis, which have not defiled
their garments: and they shall walk with me in white,
5 because they are worthy. He that shall overcome,
shall thus be clothed in white garments: and I will
not blot out his name out of the book of life: and I
will confess his name before my Father, and before his
6 angels. He that hath an ear, let him hear what the
7 Spirit saith to the churches. And to the angel of the

church of Philadelphia write: These things saith the
Holy one and the True one, who hath the key of David: He that openeth, and no man shutteth; shutteth,
8 and no man openeth: I know thy works. Behold, I
have given before thee a door opened, which no man
can shut: because thou hast a little strength, and hast
9 kept my word, and hast not denied my name. Behold,
I will bring of the synagogue of Satan, who say they
are Jews, and are not, but do lie: behold, I will make
them to come and adore before thy feet: And they
10 shall know, that I have loved thee. Because thou
hast kept the word of my patience, I will also keep
thee from the hour of temptation, which shall come
upon all the world, to tempt them that dwell upon the
11 earth. Behold, I come quickly: hold fast that which
12 thou hast, that no man take thy crown. He that shall
overcome, I will make him a pillar in the temple of
my God; and he shall go out no more: and I will
write upon him the name of my God, and the name
of the city of my God, the new Jerusalem, which
cometh down out of heaven from my God, and my new
13 name. He that hath an ear, let him hear what the
14 Spirit saith to the churches. And to the angel of the
church of Laodicia write: These things saith the
Amen, the faithful and true witness, who is the begin-
15 ning of the creation of God. I know thy works; that
thou art neither cold, nor hot: I would thou wert cold,
16 or hot: But because thou art luke-warm, and neither
cold, nor hot, I will begin to vomit thee out of my
17 mouth. Because thou sayest: I am rich, and made
wealthy, and I have need of nothing: and thou knowest not, that thou art wretched, and miserable, and
18 poor, and blind, and naked. I counsel thee to buy
of me gold tried in the fire, that thou mayest be made
rich; and mayest be clothed in white garments, that
the shame of thy nakedness may not appear: and
anoint thy eyes with eye-salve, that thou mayest see.
19 Those whom I love, I rebuke and chastise. Be zeal-
20 ous, therefore, and do penance. Behold, I stand at
the door, and knock: if any man shall hear my voice,
and open to me the gate, I will come in to him, and
21 will sup with him, and he with me. To him that shall

overcome, I will grant to sit with me in my throne: as
I also have overcome, and have sat with my Father in
22 his throne. He that hath an ear, let him hear what
the Spirit saith to the churches.

CHAP. IV. } After these things I saw: and, behold, a door
v. 1. } open in heaven: and the first voice which I
heard, *was* as it were, of a trumpet speaking with me,
saying: Come up hither, and I will show thee the
2 things which must come to pass hereafter. And immediately I was in the spirit: and, behold, there was
a throne set in heaven, and one sitting upon the throne.
3 And he that sat, was to the sight like the jasper and
the sardine-stone: and there was a rainbow round
4 about the throne, in sight like unto an emerald. And
round about the throne were four and twenty seats:
and upon the seats, four and twenty ancients sitting,
clothed in white garments, and golden crowns on their
5 heads. And from the throne proceeded lightnings,
and voices, and thunderings: and *there were* seven
lamps burning before the throne, which are the seven
6 Spirits of God. And before the throne there was as
it were a sea of glass like crystal: and in the midst
of the throne, and round about the throne *were* four
7 living creatures, full of eyes before and behind. And
the first living creature like to a lion, and the second
living creature like to a calf, and the third living creature having the face as it were, of a man: and the
fourth living creature was like to an eagle flying.
8 And the four living creatures had each of them six
wings: and round about and within they are full of
eyes. And they rested not day and night, saying,
Holy, Holy, Holy, Lord God Almighty, who was, and
9 who is, and who is to come. And when these living
creatures gave glory, and honour, and benediction to
him, that sitteth on the throne, who liveth for ever and
10 ever, The four and twenty ancients fell down before
him that sitteth on the throne, and adored him that
liveth for ever and ever, and cast their crowns before
11 the throne, saying: Thou art worthy, O Lord our
God, to receive glory, and honor, and power: because
thou hast created all things: and for thy will they
were, and have been created.

CHAP. V. } And I saw in the right hand of him that sat
v. 1. } on the throne, a book written within and with-
2 out, sealed with seven seals. And I saw a strong
angel, proclaiming with a loud voice: Who is worthy
3 to open the book, and to loose the seals thereof? And
no man was able, neither in heaven, nor in earth, nor
under the earth, to open the book, nor to look on it.
4 And I wept much, because no man was found worthy
5 to open the book, nor to see it. And one of the ancients said to me: Weep not: behold, the lion of the
tribe of Juda, the root of David, hath conquered to
open the book, and to loose the seven seals thereof.
6 And I saw: and, behold, in the midst of the throne,
and of the four living creatures, and in the midst of
the ancients, a Lamb standing as it were slain, having
seven horns and seven eyes; which are the seven
7 spirits of God, sent forth into all the earth. And he
came, and took the book out of the right hand of him
8 that sat on the throne. And when he had opened the
book, the four living creatures, and the four and twenty
ancients fell down before the Lamb, having every one
of them harps, and golden vials full of odours, which
9 are the prayers of the saints; And they sung a new
canticle, saying: Thou art worthy, O Lord, to take the
book, and to open the seals thereof: because thou
wast slain, and hast redeemed us to God, in thy blood,
out of every tribe, and tongue, and people, and na-
10 tion: And hast made us to our God a kingdom, and
11 priests: and we shall reign on the earth. And I saw,
and I heard the voice of many angels round about
the throne, and the living creatures and the ancients:
and the number of them was thousands of thousands,
12 Saying, with a loud voice: Worthy is the Lamb that
was slain, to receive power, and divinity, and wisdom,
and strength, and honour, and glory, and benediction.
13 And every creature, which is in heaven, and on the
earth, and under the earth, and such as are in the sea,
and the things that are therein: I heard all saying:
To him that sitteth on the throne, and to the Lamb,
benediction, and honour, and glory, and power, for ever
14 and ever. And the four living creatures said: Amen:
And the four and twenty ancients fell down on their
faces; and adored him that liveth for ever and ever.

CHAP. VI. } And I saw that the Lamb had opened one of
v. 1. } the seven seals: and I heard one of the four
living creatures saying, as with a voice of thunder:
2 Come thou, and see. And I saw :- and, behold, a white
horse: and he that sat on him had a bow: and a
crown was given to him: and he went forth conquer-
3 ing that he might conquer. And when he had opened
the second seal, I heard the second living creature
4 saying: Come thou, and see. And there went out
another horse that was red: and it was granted to
him who sat thereon, to take away peace from the
earth, and that they should kill one another: and to
5 him was given a great sword. And when he had
opened the third seal, I heard the third living creature saying: Come thou, and see. And, behold, a
black horse; and he that sat on him had a pair of
6 scales in his hand. And I heard as it were a voice,
in the midst of the four living creatures, saying: Two
pounds of wheat for a penny, and thrice two pounds
of barley for a penny; and wine and oil hurt thou not.
7 And when he had opened the fourth seal, I heard
the voice of the fourth living creature saying: Come
8 thou, and see. And, behold, a pale horse; and he
that sat upon him, his name was Death, and hell followed after him: and power was given to him over
the four parts of the earth, to kill with sword, with
famine, and with death, and with the beasts of the
9 earth. And when he had opened the fifth seal, I saw
under the altar the souls of them that were slain for
the word of God, and for the testimony which they
10 held. And they cried with a loud voice, saying: How
long, O Lord, (holy and true) dost thou not judge
and revenge our blood on them that dwell on the
11 earth? And white stoles were given to each of them
one: and it was said to them, that they should rest
yet for a little time, till their fellow servants, and their
brethren, who were to be slain even as they, should
12 be filled up. And I saw, when he had opened the
sixth seal: and, behold, there was a great earthquake;
and the sun became black as sackcloth of hair: and
13 the whole moon became as blood: And the stars from
heaven fell upon the earth, as the fig-tree casteth its

14 green figs when it is shaken by a great wind: And
the heaven withdrew as a book rolled up together:
and every mountain and the islands were moved out
15 of their places. And the kings of the earth, and the
princes, and the tribunes, and the rich men, and the
strong men, and every bond-man, and every free-man
hid themselves in the dens, and in the rocks of the
16 mountains: And they say to the mountains and to
the rocks: Fall upon us, and hide us from the face of
him that sitteth upon the throne, and from the wrath
17 of the Lamb: For the great day of their wrath is
come: and who shall be able to stand?

CHAP. VII. v. 1. After these things I saw four angels standing
on the four corners of the earth, holding the
four winds of the earth, that they should not blow
upon the earth, nor upon the sea, nor on any tree.
2 And I saw another angel ascending from the rising
of the sun, having the seal of the living God: and he
cried with a loud voice to the four angels, to whom it
3 was given to hurt the earth and the sea, Saying:
Hurt not the earth, nor the sea, nor the trees, till we
4 seal the servants of our God in their foreheads. And
I heard the number of them that were sealed, a hundred. forty-four thousand sealed, of all the tribes of
5 the children of Israel. Of the tribe of Juda twelve
thousand sealed: of the tribe of Ruben twelve thousand sealed: of the tribe of Gad twelve thousand sealed:
6 Of the tribe of Aser twelve thousand sealed: of the
tribe of Nephthali twelve thousand sealed: of the
7 tribe of Manasses twelve thousand sealed: Of the tribe
of Simeon twelve thousand sealed: of the tribe of
Levi twelve thousand sealed: of the tribe of Issachar
8 twelve thousand sealed: Of the tribe of Zabulon
twelve thousand sealed: of the tribe of Joseph twelve
thousand sealed: of the tribe of Benjamin twelve
9 thousand sealed. After this I saw a great multitude,
which no man could number, of all nations, and tribes,
and peoples, and tongues, standing before the throne,
and in sight of the Lamb, clothed with white robes, and
10 palms in their hands: And they cried with a loud
voice, saying: Salvation to our God, who sitteth upon

11 the throne, and to the Lamb. And all the angels
stood round about the throne, and about the ancients,
and about the four living creatures: and they fell before the throne upon their faces, and adored God,
12 Saying: Amen. Benediction, and glory, and wisdom,
and thanksgiving, honour, and power, and strength to
13 our God, for ever and ever. Amen. And one of the
ancients answered, and said to me: Who are these that
are clothed in white robes? and whence are they come?
14 And I said to him: My lord, thou knowest. And he
said to me: These are they who are come out of great
tribulation, and have washed their robes, and have
15 made them white in the blood of the Lamb. Therefore, they are before the throne of God, and serve him
day and night in his temple: and he, that sitteth on
16 the throne, shall dwell over them. They shall not
hunger, nor thirst any more; neither shall the sun fall
17 on them, nor any heat: For the Lamb, which is in the
midst of the throne, shall rule them, and shall lead
them to the fountains of the waters of life; and God
shall wipe away all tears from their eyes.

CHAP. VIII. v. 1. And when he had opened the seventh seal,
there was silence in heaven, as it were for
2 half an hour. And I saw seven angels standing in the
presence of God: and to them were given seven trum-
3 pets. And another angel came, and stood before the
altar, having a golden censer: and there was given to
him much incense, that he should offer of the prayers
of all saints upon the golden altar, which is before the
4 throne of God. And the smoke of the incense of the
prayers of the saints ascended up before God, from
5 the hand of the angel. And the angel took the censer,
and filled it with the fire of the altar, and cast it on
the earth: and there were thunderings, and voices,
6 and lightnings, and a great earthquake. And the
seven angels who had the seven trumpets, prepared
7 themselves to sound the trumpet. And the first angel
sounded the trumpet: and there was made hail, and
fire mingled with blood; and it was cast on the earth;
and the third part of the earth was burnt up, and the
third part of the trees was burnt up, and all green

8 grass was burnt up. And the second angel sounded
the trumpet: and as it were a great mountain, burning
with fire, was cast into the sea: and the third part of
9 the sea became blood. And the third part of those
creatures died, which had life in the sea: and the third
10 part of the ships was destroyed. And the third angel
sounded the trumpet: and a great star fell from heaven,
burning as it were a torch: and it fell on the third
part of the rivers, and upon the fountains of waters:
11 And the name of the star is called Wormwood: and
the third part of the waters became wormwood: and
many men died of the waters, because they were made
12 bitter. And the fourth angel sounded the trumpet:
and the third part of the sun was smitten, and the
third part of the moon, and the third part of the stars,
so that the third part of them was darkened: and the
third part of the day shined not, and of the night in
13 like manner. And I beheld, and heard the voice of
one eagle flying through the midst of heaven, saying
with a loud voice: Wo, wo, wo to the inhabitants of
the earth, by reason of the other voices of the three
angels, who are yet to sound the trumpet.

CHAP. IX. v. 1. } And the fifth angel sounded the trumpet: and
I saw a star fall from heaven upon the earth;
and to him was given the key of the bottomless pit.
2 And he opened the bottomless pit: and the smoke of
the pit ascended, as the smoke of a great furnace: and
the sun was darkened, and the air, with the smoke of
3 the pit: And from the smoke of the pit there came
out locusts upon the earth: and power was given to
4 them, as the scorpions of the earth have power: And
it was commanded them that they should not hurt the
grass of the earth, nor any green thing, nor any tree;
but only the men who have not the sign of God in their
5 foreheads: And it was given to them that they should
not kill them: but that they should torment them five
months: and their torment *was* as the torment of a
6 scorpion when he striketh a man. And in those days
men shall seek death, and shall not find it: and they
shall desire to die, and death shall fly from them.
7 And the shapes of the locusts *were* like unto horses

prepared for battle: and on their heads *were* as it were
crowns like gold; and their faces as the faces of men.
8 And they had hair as the hair of women: and their
9 teeth were as the teeth of lions: And they had breast-
plates, as it were breast-plates of iron: and the sound
of their wings *was* as the sound of chariots of many
10 horses running to battle: And they had tails like unto
scorpions, and stings were in their tails: and their
power was to hurt men five months: and they had
11 over them A king, the angel of the bottomless pit;
whose name in Hebrew, is Abaddon, and in Greek,
12 Appollyon; in Latin, Exterminans. One wo is past;
13 and, behold, there come two woes more hereafter. And
the sixth angel sounded the trumpet: and I heard a
voice from the four horns of the golden altar, which is
14 before the eyes of God, Saying to the sixth angel, who
had the trumpet: Loose the four angels, who are bound
15 in the great river Euphrates. And the four angels
were loosed, who were prepared for an hour, and a day,
and a month, and a year; for to kill the third part of
16 men. And the number of the army of horsemen was
twenty thousand times ten thousand. And I heard the
17 number of them. And thus I saw the horses in the
vision: and they who sat on them, had breast-plates
of fire, and hyacinth, and of brimstone, and the heads
of the horses were as the heads of lions: and from
their mouths proceeded fire, and smoke, and brim-
18 stone. And by these three scourges was the third
part of men killed, by the fire, and by the smoke, and
by the brimstone, which issued out of their mouths.
19 For the power of the horses is in their mouths, and in
their tails. For, their tails are like to serpents, having
20 heads; and with them they do hurt. And the rest of
the men, who were not slain by these scourges, have
not done penance for the works of their hands, that
they should not adore devils, and idols of gold and
silver and brass and stone and wood, which neither
21 can see, nor hear, nor walk: Neither have they done
penance for their murders, nor for their sorceries, nor
for their fornication, nor for their thefts.

CHAP. X. } And I saw another mighty angel come down
v. 1. } from heaven clothed with a cloud, and a rainbow upon his head; and his face was as the sun, and
2 his feet as pillars of fire: And he had in his hand
a little book open: and he set his right foot upon the
3 sea, and his left foot upon the land: And he cried out
with a loud voice, as when a lion roareth. And when
he had cried out, seven thunders uttered their voices.
4 And when the seven thunders had uttered their voices,
I was about to write: and I heard a voice from heaven,
saying to me: Seal up the things which the seven
5 thunders have spoken, and write them not. And the
angel, which I saw standing upon the sea, and upon
6 the land, lifted up his hand to heaven: And he swore
by him that liveth for ever and ever, who created
heaven, and the things which are therein; and the
earth, and the things which are therein; and the sea,
and the things which are therein: That time shall be
7 no more: But that in the days of the voice of the
seventh angel, when he shall begin to sound the trumpet, the mystery of God shall be finished, as he hath
8 declared by his servants the prophets. And I heard
a voice from heaven speaking to me again, and saying:
Go, and take the book that is open, from the hand of
the angel standing upon the sea, and upon the land.
9 And I went to the angel, saying unto him, that he
should give me the book. And he said to me: Take
the book, and devour it: and it shall make thy belly
bitter: but in thy mouth it shall be sweet as honey.
10 And I took the book from the hand of the angel, and
devoured it: and it was in my mouth sweet as honey:
11 and when I had devoured it, my belly was bitter: And
he said to me: Thou must prophecy again to nations,
and peoples, and tongues, and to many kings.

CHAP. XI. } And there was given me a reed like unto a
v. 1. } rod: and it was said to me: Rise, and measure the temple of God, and the altar, and them that
2 adore in it. But the court, which is without the temple, cast out, and measure it not, because it is given to
the Gentiles: and the holy city they shall tread under
3 foot forty-two months: And I will give to my two wit-

nesses, and they shall prophesy a thousand two hundred
4 sixty days, clothed in sackcloth. These are the two
olive-trees, and the two candlesticks, standing before
5 the Lord of the earth. And if any man would hurt
them, fire shall come out of their mouths, and shall
devour their enemies: and if any man would hurt
6 them, in this manner must he be killed. These have
power to shut heaven, that it rain not in the days of
their prophecy: and they have power over waters to
turn them into blood, and to strike the earth with all
7 plagues as often as they will. And when they shall
have finished their testimony, the beast, that ascendeth
out of the abyss, shall make war against them, and
8 shall overcome them, and kill them. And their bodies
shall lie in the streets of the great city, which spiritu-
ally is called Sodom, and Egypt, where also their Lord
9 was crucified. And they of the tribes, and peoples,
and tongues, and nations, shall see their bodies for
three days and a half; and shall not suffer their bodies
10 to be laid in sepulchres. And the inhabitants of the
earth shall rejoice over them, and make merry; and
shall send presents one to another, because these two
prophets tormented them that dwelt upon the earth.
11 And after three days and a half, the spirit of life from
God entered into them. And they stood upon their
feet: and great fear fell upon them that saw them.
12 And they heard a great voice from heaven, saying to
them: Come up hither. And they went up into heaven
13 in a cloud: and their enemies saw them. And at that
hour there was a great earthquake, and the tenth part
of the city fell: and there were slain in the earthquake,
names of men seven thousand; and the rest were cast
14 into a fear, and gave glory to the God of heaven. The
second wo is past: and, behold, the third wo will come
15 quickly. And the seventh angel sounded the trumpet:
and there were great voices in heaven, saying: The
kingdom of this world is become our Lord's and his
Christ's, and he shall reign for ever and ever: Amen.
16 And the four and twenty ancients, who sit on their
seats in the sight of God, fell upon their faces, and
17 adored God, saying: We give thee thanks, O Lord
God Almighty, who art, and who wast, and who art to

come; because thou hast taken thy great power, and
18 thou hast reigned. And the nations were angry, and
thy wrath is come, and the time of the dead to be
judged; and to render a reward to thy servants the
prophets, and to the saints, and to them that fear thy
name, little and great; and to destroy them who have
19 corrupted the earth. And the temple of God was
opened in heaven: and the ark of his testament was
seen in his temple: and there were lightnings, and
voices, and an earthquake, and great hail.

CHAP. XII. v. 1. } And there appeared a great wonder in
heaven: a woman clothed with the sun,
and the moon under her feet, and on her head a crown
2 of twelve stars: And she being with child, cried,
travailing in birth, and was in pain to be delivered.
3 And there appeared another wonder in heaven; and,
behold, a great red dragon, having seven heads, and
4 ten horns; and on his heads seven diadems. And his
tail drew the third part of the stars of heaven, and
cast them to the earth: and the dragon stood before
the woman, who was ready to be delivered; that, when
she should be delivered, he might devour her son.
5 And she brought forth a man child, who was to rule
all nations with an iron rod: and her son was taken
6 up to God, and to his throne: And the woman fled
into the wilderness, where she had a place prepared
by God, that there they should feed her a thousand
7 two hundred and sixty days. And there was a great
battle in heaven: Michael and his angels fought with
the dragon; and the dragon fought, and his angels:
8 And they prevailed not; neither was their place found
9 any more in heaven. And that great dragon was cast
out, the old serpent, who is called the devil, and Satan,
who seduceth the whole world: and he was cast forth
unto the earth; and his angels were thrown down with
10 him. And I heard a loud voice in heaven, saying:
Now is come salvation, and strength, and the kingdom
of our God, and the power of his Christ: because the
accuser of our brethren is cast forth, who accused
11 them before our God day and night. And they over-
came him by the blood of the Lamb, and by the word

of their testimony: and they loved not their lives
12 unto death. Therefore, rejoice, O ye heavens, and
you that dwell therein. Wo to the earth, and to the
sea, because the devil is come down unto you, having
great wrath, knowing that he hath *but* a short time.
13 And after the dragon saw that he was cast unto the
earth, he persecuted the woman, who brought forth
14 the man child: And there were given to the woman
two wings of a great eagle, that she might fly into the
desert to her place, where she is nourished for a time,
and times, and half a time, from the face of the ser-
15 pent. And the serpent cast out of his mouth, after the
woman, water as it were a river; that he might cause
16 her to be carried away by the river. And the earth
helped the woman; and the earth opened her mouth,
and swallowed up the river, which the dragon cast out
17 of his mouth. And the dragon was angry against the
woman; and went to make war with the rest of her
seed, which keep the commandments of God, and have
18 the testimony of Jesus Christ. And he stood upon
the sand of the sea.

CHAP. XIII. v. 1. } And I saw a beast coming out of the sea,
having seven heads and ten horns, and
upon his horns ten diadems, and upon his heads names
2 of blasphemy. And the beast, which I saw, was like
to a leopard; and his feet were as the feet of a bear,
and his mouth as the mouth of a lion. And the dragon
3 gave him his own strength, and great power. And I
saw one of his heads as it were wounded to death:
and his deadly wound was healed. And all the earth
4 was in admiration after the beast. And they adored
the dragon, which gave power to the beast: and they
adored the beast, saying: who is like to the beast?
5 and who shall be able to fight with it? And there
was given to it a mouth, speaking great things, and
blasphemies: and power was given to it to act forty-
6 two months. And he opened his mouth in blasphemies against God, to blaspheme his name, and his
7 tabernacle, and them that dwell in heaven. And it
was given to him to make war with the saints, and to
overcome them: and power was given him over every

8 tribe, and people, and tongue, and nation: And all
that dwell upon the earth, adored him; whose names
are not written in the book of life of the Lamb, which
9 was slain from the beginning of the world. If any
10 man have an ear, let him hear. He that shall lead
into captivity, shall go into captivity: he that shall
kill by the sword, must be killed by the sword. Here
11 is the patience and the faith of the saints. And I saw
another beast coming up out of the earth: and he had
two horns, like to a lamb's; and he spoke as a dragon.
12 And he executed all the power of the former beast
in his sight: and he caused the earth, and them that
dwell therein, to adore the first beast, whose deadly
13 wound was healed. And he did great signs, so that
he made even fire to come down from heaven upon
14 the earth in the sight of men. And he seduced them
that dwell on the earth, by the signs, which were given
him to perform in the sight of the beast, saying to them
that dwell on the earth, that they should make an
image to the beast, which had the wound by the sword,
15 and lived. And it was given him to give life to the
image of the beast, and that the image of the beast
should speak; and should cause, that whosoever will
not adore the image of the beast, should be slain.
16 And he shall make all, both little and great, rich and
poor, free-men and bond-men, to have a mark in their
17 right hand, or in their foreheads: And that no man
might buy or sell, but he that hath the mark, or the
18 name of the beast, or the number of his name. Here
is wisdom. He that hath understanding, let him com-
pute the number of the beast. For it is the number
of a man: and his number is six hundred sixty-six.

CHAP. XIV. v. 1. And I saw: and, behold, a Lamb stood on
mount Sion, and with him a hundred forty-
four thousand having his name and the name of his
2 Father written in their foreheads. And I heard a
voice from heaven, as the voice of many waters, and
as the voice of great thunder: and the voice which I
3 heard, was as of harpers, harping on their harps. And
they sung as it were a new canticle, before the throne,
and before the four living creatures, and the ancients:

and no man could say the canticle, but those hundred
forty-four thousand, who were purchased from the
4 earth. These are they who were not defiled with women: for they are virgins. These follow the Lamb
withersoever he goeth. These were purchased from
among men, the first fruits to God, and to the Lamb:
5 And in their mouth was found no lie: for they are
6 without spot before the throne of God. And I saw
another angel flying through the midst of heaven, having the eternal gospel, to preach to them that sit upon
the earth, and over every nation, and tribe, and tongue,
7 and people: Saying with a loud voice: Fear the
Lord, and give him honour; because the hour of his
judgment is come: and adore ye him, who made
heaven, and earth, the sea, and the fountains of waters.
8 And another angel followed, saying: She is fallen, she
is fallen, that great Babylon; which made all nations
9 drink of the wine of the wrath of her fornication. And
the third angel followed them, saying with a loud
voice: If any man shall adore the beast, and his
image, and receive his mark in his forehead, or in his
10 hand: He also shall drink of the wine of the wrath
of God, which is mingled with pure wine, in the cup
of his wrath: and he shall be tormented with fire and
brimstone in the sight of the holy angels, and in the
11 sight of the Lamb: And the smoke of their torments
shall ascend up for ever and ever: neither have they
rest day nor night, who have adored the beast, and his
image, and whosoever did receive the mark of his name.
12 Here is the patience of the saints, who keep the com-
13 mandments of God, and the faith of Jesus. And I
heard a voice from heaven, saying to me: Write:
Blessed are the dead, who die in the Lord. From
henceforth now, saith the Spirit, that they may rest
14 from their labours: for their works follow them. And
I saw: and, behold, a white cloud, and upon the cloud
one sitting like to the Son of man, having on his head
15 a golden crown, and in his hand a sharp sickle. And
another angel came out of the temple, crying with a
loud voice to him that sat upon the cloud: Put to thy
sickle, and reap, because the hour is come to reap; for
16 the harvest of the earth is ripe. And he that sat on

the cloud, put his sickle to the earth; and the earth
17 was reaped. And another angel came out of the temple, which is in heaven, he also having a sharp sickle.
18 And another angel came out from the altar, who had
power over fire: and he cried with a loud voice to him
that had the sharp sickle, saying: Put to thy sharp
sickle, and gather the clusters of the vineyard of the
19 earth; because the grapes thereof are ripe. And the
angel put his sharp sickle to the earth, and gathered
the vineyard of the earth, and cast it into the great
20 wine-press of the wrath of God: And the wine-press
was trodden without the city: and blood came out of
the wine-press, even up to the horses' bridles, for a
thousand and six hundred furlongs.

CHAP. XV. v. 1. } And I saw another sign in heaven, great
and wonderful, seven angels having the
seven last plagues: for in them is filled up the wrath
2 of God. And I saw as it were a sea of glass mingled
with fire, and them that had overcome the beast, and
his image, and the number of his name, standing on
3 the sea of glass, having the harps of God: And sing-
ing the canticle of Moses the servant of God, and the
canticle of the Lamb, saying: Great and wonderful
are thy works, O Lord God Almighty: just and true
4 are thy ways, O King of ages. Who shall not fear
thee, O Lord, and magnify thy name? For thou only
art holy: for all nations shall come, and shall adore in
5 thy sight; because thy judgments are manifest. And
after these things I saw: and, behold, the temple of
the tabernacle of the testimony in heaven was opened:
6 And the seven angels came out of the temple, having
the seven plagues, clothed in clean and white linen,
and girded about the breasts with golden girdles.
7 And one of the four living creatures gave to the seven
angels seven golden vials, full of the wrath of God,
8 who liveth for ever and ever. And the temple was
filled with smoke from the majesty of God, and from
his power: and no man was able to enter into the temple, till the seven plagues of the seven angels were
fulfilled.

CHAP. XVI. } And I heard a great voice out of the tem-
v. 1. } ple, saying to the seven angels: Go, and
pour out the seven vials of the wrath of God upon the
2 earth. And the first went, and poured out his vial
upon the earth: and there fell a sore and most griev-
ous wound upon the men, who had the mark of the
3 beast, and upon them who adored his image. And
the second angel poured out his vial into the sea: and
it became as the blood of a dead man: and every
4 living soul died in the sea. And the third poured
out his vial upon the rivers, and the fountains of wa-
5 ters: and they became blood. And I heard the angel
of the waters, saying: Thou art just, O Lord, who
art, and who wast the holy one, who hast judged these
6 things: For they have shed the blood of the saints
and prophets; and thou hast given them blood to
7 drink: for they deserved it. And I heard another
from the altar, saying: Yea, O Lord God Almighty,
8 true and just *are* thy judgments. And the fourth
angel poured out his vial upon the sun: and it was
9 given to him to afflict men with heat and fire: And
men were scorched with great heat: and they blasphemed the name of God, who hath power over these
plagues; neither did they penance to give him glory.
10 And the fifth angel poured out his vial upon the seat
of the beast: and his kingdom became dark; and they
11 gnawed their tongues for pain: And they blasphemed
the God of heaven, because of their pains, and wounds,
12 and did not penance for their works. And the sixth
angel poured out his vial upon that great river Euphrates; and dried up the water thereof, that a way
might be prepared for the kings from the rising of the
13 sun. And I saw from the mouth of the dragon, and
from the mouth of the beast, and from the mouth of
14 the false prophet, three unclean spirits like frogs. For
they are the spirits of devils working signs: and they
go forth unto the kings of the whole earth to gather
them to battle against the great day of the Almighty
15 God. Behold, I come as a thief. Blessed is he that
watcheth and keepeth his garments, lest he walk naked,
16 and they see his shame. And he shall gather them
together into a place, which is called in Hebrew

17 Armagedon. And the seventh angel poured out his
vial into the air: and a great voice came out of the
18 temple from the throne, saying: It is done. And
there were lightnings, and voices, and thunders: and
there was a great earthquake, such as never hath been
since men were upon the earth; such an earthquake,
19 so great. And the great city was made into three
parts: and the cities of the Gentiles fell; and great
Babylon came in remembrance before God, to give to
her the cup of the wine of the indignation of his wrath.
20 And every island fled away, and the mountains were
21 not found. And great hail like a talent came down
from heaven upon men: and men blasphemed God
because of the plague of the hail; for it was exceeding great.

CHAP. XVII. v. 1. And there came one of the seven angels,
who had the seven vials, and spoke with
me, saying: Come, I will show thee the condemnation
of the great harlot, who sitteth upon many waters.
2 With whom the kings of the earth have committed
fornication: and they who inhabit the earth, have been
3 made drunk with the wine of her prostitution. And
he took me away in the spirit into the desert. And
I saw a woman sitting upon a scarlet-coloured beast,
full of names of blasphemy, having seven heads and
4 ten horns. And the woman was clothed round in
purple and scarlet, and gilded with gold, and precious
stones and pearls, having a golden cup in her hand,
full of the abomination and filthiness of her fornica-
5 tion. And on her forehead a name was written: A
mystery: Babylon the great, the mother of the for-
6 nications and abominations of the earth. And I saw
the woman drunk with the blood of the saints, and
with the blood of the martyrs of Jesus. And when I
7 had seen her, I wondered with great admiration. And
the angel said to me: Why dost thou wonder? I
will tell thee the mystery of the woman, and of the
beast which carrieth her, which hath the seven heads
8 and ten horns. The beast, which thou sawest, was,
and is not, and shall come up out of the bottomless
pit, and go into destruction: and the inhabitants of the

earth (whose names are not written in the book of life
from the foundation of the world) shall wonder seeing
9 the beast, that was, and is not. And here is the
understanding, that hath wisdom. The seven heads
are seven mountains, upon which the woman sitteth,
10 and they are seven kings: Five are fallen; one is;
and the other is not yet come: and when he shall
11 come, he must remain a short time. And the beast
that was, and is not; the same is also the eighth, and
12 is of the seven, and goeth into destruction. And the
ten horns, which thou sawest, are ten kings; who have
not yet received a kingdom, but shall receive power
13 as kings one hour after the beast. These have one
design; and their strength and power they shall de-
14 liver to the beast. They shall fight with the Lamb;
and the Lamb shall overcome them; because he is
Lord of lords, and King of kings; and they that are
15 with him are called, and elect, and faithful. And he
said to me: The waters which thou sawest, where the
harlot sitteth, are peoples, and nations, and tongues.
16 And the ten horns, which thou sawest on the beast;
these shall hate the harlot, and shall make her desolate and naked, and shall eat her flesh, and shall burn
17 her with fire. For God hath given into their hearts,
to do that which pleaseth him; that they give their
kingdom to the beast till the words of God be fulfilled.
18 And the woman which thou sawest, is the great city,
a kingdom which hath dominion over the kings of the
earth.

CHAP. XVIII. v. 1. } And after these things I saw another angel
coming down from heaven, having great
power: and the earth was enlightened with his glory.
2 And he cried out with a strong voice, saying: Babylon
the great is fallen, is fallen; and is become the habitation of devils, and the hold of every unclean spirit,
3 and the hold of every unclean and hateful bird: Because all nations have drunk of the wine of the wrath
of her fornication: and the kings of the earth have
committed fornication with her: and the merchants of
the earth have been made rich by the abundance of
4 her delicacies. And I heard another voice from heaven,

saying: Go out from her, my people; that you be not
partakers of her sins, and that you receive not of her
5 plagues. For her sins have reached even to heaven:
6 and the Lord hath remembered her iniquities. Render to her as she also hath rendered to you: and double
ye the double according to her works: in the cup,
wherein she hath mingled, mingle unto her double.
7 As much as she hath glorified herself, and hath been
in delicacies, so much torment and sorrow give unto
her: because she saith in her heart: I sit a queen,
8 and am not a widow; and sorrow I shall not see. Therefore shall her plagues come in one day, death, and
mourning, and famine: and she shall be burnt with
9 fire; because God is strong, who shall judge her. And
the kings of the earth, who have committed fornication, and lived in delicacies with her, shall weep, and
bewail themselves over her, when they shall see the
10 smoke of her burning: Standing afar off for fear of
her torments, saying: Wo, wo that great city Babylon,
that mighty city: for in one hour is thy judgment
11 come. And the merchants of the earth shall weep,
and mourn over her: for no man shall buy their mer-
12 chandise any more: Merchandise of gold, and silver,
and of precious stones, and pearl, and of fine linen,
and purple, and of silk, and scarlet (and all thyine
wood, and all manner of vessels of ivory, and all manner of vessels of precious stone, and of brass, and iron,
13 and marble, And cinnamon) and of odours, and ointment, and frankincense, and wine, and oil, and fine
flour, and wheat, and beasts, and sheep, and horses,
14 and chariots, and slaves, and souls of men. And the
fruits of the desire of thy soul are departed from thee;
and all fat and goodly things are perished from thee;
15 and they shall no more find them. The merchants of
these things, who were made rich, shall stand afar off
from her, for fear of her torments, weeping and mourn-
16 ing, And saying: Wo, wo that great city, which was
clothed with fine linen, and purple, and scarlet, and
was gilded with gold and precious stones and pearls:
17 For in one hour are so great riches come to nothing:
and every ship-master, and every one that sails into
the lake, and mariners, and they that work at sea,

18 stood afar off; And cried out, seeing the place of her
burning, saying: What city *is* like to this great city?
19 And they cast dust upon their heads, and cried out,
weeping and mourning, saying: Wo, wo that great
city, wherein all were made rich, who had ships at sea,
by reason of her prices: for in one hour she is made
20 desolate. Rejoice over her, thou heaven, and ye holy
apostles, and prophets: for God hath judged your
21 judgment on her. And a mighty angel took up a
stone as it were a great mill-stone, and cast it into the
sea, saying: With this violence shall Babylon, that
great city, be thrown down, and shall now be found
22 no more. And the voice of harpers, and of musicians,
and of them that play on the pipe, and on the trumpet,
shall no more be heard in thee: and no craftsman
of any art whatsoever shall be found any more in
thee: and the sound of a mill shall be heard no more
23 in thee: And the light of a lamp shall shine no more
in thee: and the voice of the bridegroom and bride
shall be heard no more in thee: for thy merchants
were the great men of the earth, for all nations have
24 been deceived by thy sorceries. And in her hath been
found the blood of prophets and of saints, and of all,
who were slain upon the earth.

CHAP. XIX. v. 1. After these things I heard as it were the
voice of many multitudes in heaven, saying:
Alleluia: salvation, and glory, and power is to
2 our God: For true and just are his judgments, who
hath judged the great harlot, which corrupted the
earth with her fornication, and hath revenged the
3 blood of his servants, at her hands. And again they
said: Alleluia. And her smoke ascendeth for ever
4 and ever. And the four and twenty ancients, and the
four living creatures fell down and adored God that
5 sitteth upon the throne, saying: Amen: Alleluia. And
a voice came out from the throne, saying: Praise ye
our God all his servants, and you that fear him, little
6 and great. And I heard as it were the voice of a
great multitude, and as the voice of many waters, and
as the voice of great thunders, saying: Alleluia: for
7 the Lord our God the omnipotent hath reigned. Let

us be glad, and rejoice, and give glory to him: for the
marriage of the Lamb is come, and his wife hath pre-
8 pared herself. And to her it hath been granted, that
she should clothe herself with fine linen, glittering and
white. For the fine linen are the justifications of
9 saints. And he saith to me: Write: Blessed are they,
who are called to the marriage supper of the Lamb:
and he saith to me: These words of God are true.
10 And I fell before his feet to adore him. And he saith
to me: see thou do it not: I am thy fellow-servant,
and of thy brethren who have the testimony of Jesus.
Adore God. For the testimony of Jesus is the spirit
11 of prophecy. And I saw heaven opened, and, behold,
a white horse: and he that sat upon him, was called
Faithful and True; and with justice he judgeth and
12 fighteth. And his eyes *were* as a flame of fire, and
on his head many diadems, having a name written,
13 which no man knoweth but himself. And he was
clothed with a garment sprinkled with blood: and his
14 name is called, THE WORD OF GOD. And the
armies which are in heaven followed him on white
15 horses, clothed in fine linen white and clean. And out
of his mouth proceedeth a sharp two-edged sword;
that with it he may strike the Gentiles. And he shall
rule them with a rod of iron: and he treadeth the
wine-press of the fury of the wrath of God the Al-
16 mighty. And he hath on his garment and on his
17 thigh written: King of kings, and Lord of lords. And
I saw an angel standing in the sun: and he cried with
a loud voice, saying to all the birds that did fly through
the midst of heaven: Come, and gather yourselves
18 together to the great supper of God: That you may
eat the flesh of kings, and the flesh of tribunes, and
the flesh of mighty men, and the flesh of horses, and
of them that sit on them, and the flesh of all free-men
19 and bond-men, and of little and great. And I saw
the beast, and the kings of the earth and their armies
gathered together to make war with him that sat upon
20 the horse, and with his army. And the beast was
taken, and with him the false prophet; who wrought
signs before him, wherewith he seduced them, who received the mark of the beast, and who adored his

image. These two were cast alive into the pool of
21 fire burning with brimstone. And the rest were slain
by the sword of him that sitteth upon the horse, which
proceedeth out of his mouth: and all the birds were
filled with their flesh.

CHAP. XX. v. 1. } And I saw an angel coming down from
heaven, having the key of the bottomless
2 pit, and a great chain in his hand. And he laid hold
on the dragon, the old serpent, which is the devil and
3 Satan, and bound him for a thousand years: And
he cast him into the bottomless pit, and shut him up,
and set a seal upon him, that he should no more seduce
the nations, till the thousand years be finished: and
4 after that he must be loosed a little time. And I saw
seats, and they sat upon them: and judgment was
given unto them: and the souls of them that were be-
headed for the testimony of Jesus, and for the word of
God, and who had not adored the beast, nor his image,
nor received his mark in their foreheads, or in their
hands: and they lived and reigned with Christ a
5 thousand years. The rest of the dead lived not, till
the thousand years were finished. This is the first
6 resurrection. Blessed and holy is he that hath part
in the first resurrection: in these the second death hath
no power: but they shall be priests of God and of
Christ, and shall reign with him a thousand years.
7 And when the thousand years shall be finished, Satan
shall be loosed out of his prison, and shall go forth,
and seduce the nations, which are over the four quar-
ters of the earth, Gog, and Magog, and shall gather
them together to battle, whose number is as the sand
8 of the sea. And they ascended upon the breadth of
the earth, and surrounded the camp of the saints, and
9 the beloved city. And fire came down from God out
of heaven, and devoured them: and the devil, who
seduced them, was cast into the pool of fire and brim-
10 stone, where both the beast And the false prophet
shall be tormented day and night for ever and ever.
11 And I saw a great white throne, and him that sat
upon it, from whose presence the earth and heaven
fled away, and there was no place found for them.

12 And I saw the dead great and small, standing before
the throne; and the books were opened: and another
book was opened, which is *the book* of life; and the
dead were judged by those things which were written
13 in the books, according to their works. And the sea
gave up the dead, that were in it: and death and hell
gave up their dead, that were in them: and they were
14 judged every one according to their works. And hell
and death were cast into the pool of fire. This is the
15 second death. And whosoever was not found written
in the book of life, was cast into the pool of fire.

CHAP. XXI. } And I saw a new heaven, and a new earth.
v. 1. } For the first heaven and the first earth
2 was passed away; and the sea is no more. And I
John saw the holy city the new Jerusalem coming
down from God out of heaven, prepared as a bride
3 adorned for her husband. And I heard a great voice
from the throne, saying: Behold the tabernacle of God
with men; and he will dwell with them: And they
shall be his people: and God himself with them shall
4 be their God: And God shall wipe away all tears
from their eyes: and death shall be no more; nor
mourning, nor crying, nor sorrow shall be any more;
5 for the former things are passed away. And he who
sat on the throne, said: Behold, I make all things
new. And he said to me; Write, for these words are
6 most faithful and true. And he said to me: It is done:
I am alpha and omega; the beginning and the end.
To him that thirsteth I will give of the fountain of the
7 water of life, gratis. He that shall overcome, shall
possess these things: and I will be his God, and he
8 shall be my son. But to the fearful, and unbelieving,
and the abominable, and murderers, and fornicators,
and sorcerers, and idolaters, and all liars, their portion
shall be in the pool burning with fire and brimstone;
9 which is the second death. And there came one of
the seven angels, who had the vials full of the seven
last plagues, and spoke with me, saying: Come, and
10 I will show thee the bride, the wife of the Lamb. And
he took me up in spirit to a great and high mountain:
and he showed me the holy city Jerusalem, coming

11 down out of heaven from God, Having the glory of
God; and the light thereof like unto a precious stone,
12 as it were to a jasper-stone, as crystal. And it had a
wall great and high, having twelve gates; and in the
gates twelve angels, and names written thereon, which
are the names of the twelve tribes of the children of
13 Israel. On the east, three gates; and on the north,
three gates; and on the south, three gates; and on
14 the west, three gates. And the wall of the city had
twelve foundations; and in them, the twelve names
15 of the twelve apostles of the Lamb. And he that
spoke with me, had a measure, a golden reed, to
measure the city and the gates thereof, and the wall.
16 And the city is situate four-square; and the length
thereof is as great as the breadth: and he measured
the city with a golden reed for twelve thousand furlongs: and the length, and the height, and the breadth
17 of it are equal. And he measured the wall thereof
a hundred forty-four cubits, the measure of a man,
18 which is of an angel. And the building of the wall
thereof was of jasper-stone: but the city itself pure
19 gold, like to clear glass. And the foundations of the
wall of the city were adorned with all manner of precious stones. The first foundation, jasper: the second,
sapphire: the third, a calcedony: the fourth, an em-
20 erald: The fifth, sardonyx: the sixth, sardius: the
seventh, crysolite: the eighth, beryl: the ninth, a
topaz: the tenth, a chrysoprasus: the eleventh, a
21 jacinth: the twelfth, an amethyst. And the twelve
gates are twelve pearls, one to each: and every several
gate was of one several pearl: and the street of the
22 city was pure gold, as it were transparent glass. And
I saw no temple in it. For the Lord God Almighty
23 is the temple thereof, and the Lamb. And the city
needeth not sun nor moon to shine in it: for the glory
of God hath enlightened it: and the Lamb is the lamp
24 thereof. And nations shall walk in the light of it:
and the kings of the earth shall bring their glory
25 and honour into it. And the gates thereof shall not
be shut by day: for there shall be no night there.
26 And they shall bring the glory and honour of the na-
27 tions into it. There shall not enter into it any thing

defiled, or any one that worketh abomination, or a lie; but they who are written in the book of life of the Lamb.

CHAP. XXII. } And he showed me a river of water of life,
v. 1. } clear as crystal, proceeding from the throne
2 of God, and of the Lamb. In the midst of the street
thereof, and on both sides of the river, *was* the tree of
life, bearing twelve fruits, yielding its fruit every
month, and the leaves of the tree for the healing of the
3 nations. And no curse shall be any more: but the
throne of God, and of the Lamb shall be in it; and
4 his servants shall serve him. And they shall see his
5 face: and his name shall be on their foreheads. And
night shall be no more: and they shall not need the
light of a lamp, nor the light of the sun; for the Lord
God shall enlighten them; and they shall reign for
6 ever and ever. And he said to me: These words are
most faithful and true. And the Lord God of the
spirits of the prophets sent his angel to show his ser-
7 vants the things which must be done shortly. And,
behold, I come quickly. Blessed is he that keepeth
8 the words of the prophecy of this book. And I John,
who have heard and seen these things. And after I
had heard and seen, I fell down to adore before the
9 feet of the angel, who showed me these things: And
he said to me: See thou do *it* not: for I am thy fellow-
servant, and of thy brethren the prophets, and of them
who keep the words of the prophecy of this book:
10 Adore God. And he saith to me: Seal not the words
of the prophecy of this book: for the time is at hand.
11 He that hurteth, let him hurt still: and he that is filthy,
let him be filthy still: and he that is just, let him be
justified still: and he that is holy, let him be sancti-
12 fied still. Behold, I come quickly: and my reward is
with me, to render to every man according to his works.
13 I am alpha, and omega, the first, and the last, the be-
14 ginning, and the end. Blessed are they that wash their
robes in the blood of the Lamb; that they may have
a right to the tree of life, and may enter in by the
15 gates into the city. Without *are* dogs, and sorcerers,
and the unchaste, and murderers, and those that serve

16 idols, and every one that loveth and maketh a lie. I
Jesus have sent my angel, to testify to you these things
in the churches. I am the root and stock of David,
17 the bright and morning star. And the Spirit and the
bride say: Come. And he that heareth, let him say:
Come. And he that thirsteth, let him come: and he
18 that will, let him take the water of life, gratis. For I
testify to every one that heareth the words of the
prophecy of this book: If any man shall add to these
things, God shall add upon him the plagues written
19 in this book. And if any man shall take away from
the words of the book of this prophecy, God shall
take away his part out of the book of life, and out of
the holy city, and from these things which are written
20 in this book. He that giveth testimony of these things,
saith: Surely I come quickly: Amen. Come, Lord
21 Jesus. The grace of our Lord Jesus Christ be with
you all. Amen.

www.ingramcontent.com/pod-product-compliance
Lightning Source LLC
LaVergne TN
LVHW021415110826
845150LV00007B/1931

* 9 7 8 1 4 2 5 5 1 0 6 2 6 *